Haircuts and Holiness

Haircuts and Holiness

Discussion Starters for Religious Encounter Groups

Louis Cassels

Abingdon Press - Nashville - New York

HAIRCUTS AND HOLINESS

Copyright © 1972 by Louis Cassels

ISBN 0-687-16475-3

Library of Congress Catalog Card Number: 76-172817

The prayer by John Baillie is reprinted by permission of Charles Scribner's Sons from *A Diary of Private Prayer*, p. 15, by John Baillie. Copyright 1949 by Charles Scribner's Sons.

Scripture quotations from the Old Testament are from the Revised Standard Version of the Bible, copyrighted 1946 and 1952 by the Division of Christian Education, National Council of Churches, and are used by permission.

Scripture quotations from the New Testament are from *Good News for Modern Man*, Today's English Version of the New Testament, copyrighted 1966 by the American Bible Society.

MANUFACTURED BY THE PARTHENON PRESS AT
NASHVILLE, TENNESSEE, UNITED STATES OF AMERICA

To Rachel Lyman

In grateful and affectionate recognition of her indispensable assistance with all my books, and in frank admiration of the most generous Christian spirit I've ever encountered

Contents

"Let us, you and I, lay aside all arrogance. Let neither of us pretend to have found the truth. Let us seek it as something unknown to both of us. Then we may seek it with love and sincerity, when neither of us has the rashness or presumption to believe that he already possesses it."

—St. Augustine

☀ A Preliminary Word to the Reader

About the purpose and content of this book

Some people are content to base their religious decisions on information, attitudes, and viewpoints spoon-fed to them in sermons and Sunday school lessons. If they find the diet palatable, they keep coming back for more. If they can't swallow what's set before them in the church they happen to attend, they reject the whole religious enterprise, never bothering to inquire whether it was real Christianity or a pathetic caricature which put them off.

If you are satisfied with such a passive-reactive approach to the ultimate questions of human existence, you may as well return this book right now and get your money back. For my

9

sole purpose will be to encourage, challenge, stimulate, or irritate you into doing your own thinking about such things as whether it is reasonable to believe in God, how (if at all) we can gain reliable knowledge of him, and what (if anything) he requires of us.

I have been wrestling with these questions for a great many years and have arrived at certain convictions which I intend to share with you as honestly and forthrightly as possible. I'll also quote other people whose opinions make sense to me. But I neither want nor expect you to accept these views unless, after thoughtful consideration, you find they make sense to you too.

To avoid monotonous repetition, I shan't preface every sentence with "in my opinion," or "I believe," or "it seems to me." But I hope you'll consider these disavowals of omniscience to be implicit in all my statements, even those which may sound a mite positive.

A wise editor once told me that a writer should strive not to make up but to shake up the minds of readers. This seems to me particularly necessary in dealing with religious questions, for no one can be said really to believe something until he has doubted it enough to subject it to serious questioning.

So, I repeat, if you want your brain washed, you'll have to go elsewhere. All we're peddling at this stand is provocation.

If you decide to remain aboard, you will find in the pages that follow a series of brief discourses or dissertations or essays or meditations—I really don't know what to call them. They will vary in length from as little as 500 words to as much as 2,000 words, but none of them will require more than a few minutes of reading time.

I hope, however, that they will induce a great deal more than a few minutes of thinking and pondering time. At the end of each I will raise a few questions which seem to me worth meditation or discussion. But these are purely suggestions, and if your mind takes off on a different track, by all means let it run.

My primary idea was that this little book might be useful in providing common starting ground for small, informal discussion groups meeting in someone's living room.

In recent years, a spontaneous movement has developed in many denominations and in all parts of the country to form small discussion groups of "prayer cells" in which concerned Christian laymen can share intimately and honestly their religious insights, doubts, problems, and experiences. This is one of the most vital signs of genuine renewal in the church today. It can, as some groups I know have demonstrated, lead to the same deep sense of oneness-in-Christ that was such a vivid force in the "house churches" of first-century Christianity. It was precisely to such groups as these that the guidance of the Holy Spirit was promised—and abundantly manifested.

Perhaps you're already involved in, or at least familiar with, such a group. If you are not, and would like to set one up, here are a few suggestions on how to go about it. These are intended only as a starting point. Obviously, you'll develop your own detailed ideas about organization and procedure as you go along.

As a general rule, I think it's a good idea to meet once a week, on a fixed evening. It is essential that the group be kept small enough for intimate discussion, which means that a dozen people is just about the maximum.

It also is very important that every member of the group prepare for the discussion in advance by reading and pondering the material which has been chosen for that week. That's where this book comes in. But if you find that you aren't stimulated by what I have to say, or if you run through the material in this book and need more, I'm sure that with a little exploration you can find other books to discuss chapter by chapter.

You'll probably need a moderator to keep the discussion

11

on the track and discourage filibusters. But his or her leader-
ship should be unobtrusive and the dialogue should be as
free and informal as possible. It will help if each participant
will bear in mind that no one is there to sell his ideas to someone else. Your purpose is to think, learn, and care together.

I strongly recommend that each meeting begin with a prayer
for presence and guidance of the Holy Spirit. This is not just
a pious convention. The Holy Spirit is very real indeed, as
you will find out if you seriously ask him to take charge not
only of your discussions but of your life.

If you are unable to form a group, or if you feel tempera-
mentally unsuited to group discussion, there is an alternative
way in which you can use this book: as an aid to private
meditation. Set aside a definite time each week. An hour that
you can be reasonably sure of safeguarding from intrusion or
interruption will be ample. Read *one* section a week—not
more. Then ponder and pray over the ideas, questions, or
claims which you encountered in the text, as well as others
that come to your mind through association.

In private meditation as well as group discussion, one
should always begin by asking the Holy Spirit to communicate
his truth to you, through this reading and thinking process.
Although his communications sometimes are quite dramatic,
you should not count on or consciously strive for any overt or
ecstatic manifestations of his presence.

To most people, most of the time, the "voice" of the Holy
Spirit consists of a silent guidance of mind, will, and feelings.
Only in retrospect, usually, are we aware that we have been
made wiser, better, and stronger by a power from beyond
ourselves.

1 ☀ Haircuts and Holiness

There is a verse of scripture which every parent should commit to memory.

It's found in the Old Testament in the sixteenth chapter of the first book of Samuel:

"The Lord sees not as a man sees. Man looks on the outward appearance, but the Lord looks on the heart."

Many a harsh family row might be avoided if parents could learn to look on their children as the Lord does: focusing not on the outward appearance, but on the heart.

Being bald and middle-aged, I have no difficulty understanding why people of my generation are put off by some of the hair styles and clothing now in vogue among young people.

What I cannot comprehend is why otherwise-intelligent adults should attach such overriding importance to what is, after all, a question of taste, not a basic moral issue.

I vividly remember an occasion when a United States Congressman learned that his son had been arrested and jailed on a charge of marijuana possession. In a statement to the press at the time that he posted $2,500 bond to secure his nineteen-year-old son's release from jail, the Congressman said he had told his son, "I'll give you one chance, and give you written conditions. If you break them, I'll put you back in jail."

And what were the written conditions? The lawmaker listed them as follows:

His son must "get his hair cut, and short, and now."

He must "keep himself shaved."

He must "visit a professional barber" at least once every ten days.

He must not "wear hippie clothes."

He must return to school (from which he had dropped out two years previously).

He must avoid use of drugs.

No parent could quarrel with the last two admonitions— that the young man go back to school and lay off drugs. They are clearly aimed at protecting his welfare in essential respects.

But note, please, that the first four of the six "written conditions" were entirely concerned with the youth's outward appearance.

It staggers credulity that it should be necessary to point it out, but perhaps it is necessary: long hair is neither more nor less moral, neither more nor less acceptable in the sight of God, neither more nor less manly if you want to put it on that basis, than short hair, or no hair at all.

There may be some validity to the widely held adult belief that children tend to behave as they dress—that is, to live up to the roles for which they are costumed. To the degree that is true, it would be a legitimate basis for some concern about teen-age hairdos and clothing fads.

But any trouble a child is apt to get into from dressing up like a hippie is not a patch on the disasters that can result from total estrangement from his parents.

When young people see their parents making a big fuss over a superficial and relatively trivial thing, such as hair

14

length, they find it difficult to take seriously the other "values" which their parents commend to them.

Much better a long-haired, well-loved child than one who has a neat crewcut and a heart full of bitterness.

★ Questions to ponder or discuss

How did Jesus wear his hair? Was he clean-shaven?

Why, in your opinion, has hair become the preeminent symbol of generational conflict in our time?

Do young people bear some responsibility for the "uptightness" of many adults over long hair?

2 ✸ Barriers to Belief

When people say God is dead, what they really mean is that the idea of God has ceased to be credible for large numbers of men and women.

This is undeniably true. But it should be borne in mind that this is a statement about the mental attitude of modern man—not about the reality of God.

"The reality of God is not affected by whether or not I am aware of his presence," says Robert McAfee Brown, professor of religion at Stanford University. "The fact that I don't see the sun at any given moment doesn't mean it is not there. My eyes may be closed. There maybe heavy clouds. Or I may be looking in the wrong direction."

No one can prove by logical argument that God does in fact exist. On the other hand, no one can prove the non-existence of God. We are faced with a choice between two hypotheses, either of which can be defended intellectually, neither of which can be proved.

"God is, or he is not," said Blaise Pascal, the great scientist-philosopher of seventeenth-century France. "To which side shall we incline? Reason can settle nothing here. You must wager."

Some try to avoid the wager by saying that the evidence is insufficient for a rational decision. But that is precisely Pascal's point. However attractive agnosticism may seem as an intellectual stance, it is hard to remain permanently in a state of indecision about the existence of God. Each day, you are compelled to make decisions about how you'll act and which values you'll put first. And these practical decisions are necessarily based on some assumption about the meaning of life. Willy-nilly, you act *as though* God were real, or *as though* God were an irrelevant fiction. As the late Harry Emerson Fosdick put it, "You can avoid making up your mind, but you cannot avoid making up your life."

So Pascal was right. There is no way to cop out. Either God is or he is not, and each of us bets his life on one proposition or the other. It is the most important decision we have to make, for it ultimately determines our attitude toward everything else.

In making this decision, you should bear one very important fact in mind:

As an educated person of our time, you are inevitably biased *against* belief in God, whether you realize it or not.

Several factors have helped to create our built-in bias against belief.

One is the awe in which physical science is held by many laymen. Every age has its superstitions, and ours is the notion that science is an infallible and all-sufficient guide to truth. The corollary is that the only kind of reality worth bothering about is that which can be verified by the methods of physical science.

Scientists, if consulted, would vigorously refute this idea. They are keenly aware that science itself depends on essentially metaphysical postulates—such as the order and intelligibility of the natural universe—which cannot be verified by scientific methods but must be accepted, so to speak, on faith. "Science is impossible without faith—the faith that

17

nature is subject to law," says Norbert Wiener, the father of cybernetics.

Another widely encountered barrier to belief is the cynicism many of us have developed in response to attempts by advertisers, politicians, and other hidden persuaders to manipulate our thinking. We've been deceived, manipulated, managed, and misled so often we have little capacity left for believing anything.

When skepticism becomes an automatic reflex action, it is as poor a guide to truth as naïve credulity.

A third aspect of contemporary culture which militates against belief in God is our preoccupation with secular concerns. Our secularity is in part a product of affluence. We are swamped by *things*, which must be bought, paid for, used, repaired, remodeled, and replaced. We possess them—and are possessed by them.

But secularity also is in part the result of a nobler characteristic which is quite commonplace today, especially among young people. This is a commitment to the eradication of injustice and gross inequality in society. To say that this is a secular goal is not to suggest that it is in any way contrary to God's will. I am personally convinced that just the opposite is true. But because it focuses our attention on the here-and-now world of material needs and human interrelationships, it can be—and for many has been—a distraction from any serious consideration of the God-question.

Our bias against belief operates in insidious ways. Although modern scholarship has made us aware of the extent to which the beliefs of men in previous ages were affected by the cultural assumptions of their time, we rarely take account of the fact that our beliefs also are conditioned, and in some cases dictated, by unexamined attitudes which we have simply absorbed from our surrounding culture.

It is necessary that we fully recognize this truth. For there surely can be nothing more arrogant—or more irrational—

than to judge the truth or falsity of any idea solely on the basis of whether it happens to be congenial to the mind-set of our particular generation.

★ Questions to ponder or discuss

Can you think of any other elements of contemporary culture which serve as barriers to belief?

Do you find it easier to hold to beliefs which are socially reinforced by the attitudes of those around you than to retain beliefs which are widely derided as outmoded, "superstitious," or "unscientific"?

Has your own belief in God been shaken by a suspicion that even some clergymen and theologians now regard theism as passé?

3 ☀ The Impact of Modern Science on Belief

One of the universal traits of human beings, psychologists say, is a drive to *understand*.

The desire to make sense out of the world is distinctive to our species. It is not shared by other animals. A cat or dog may display curiosity about a specific object or event. But man's quest for comprehension goes far beyond mere curiosity. He wants to know *why* things are as they are. He gropes for relationships, seeks to identify causes and effects. He often has to settle for partial explanations, but is never fully satisfied with them.

As long as man-the-inquirer focuses his attention on secondary causes, he is neither inhibited nor helped by a philosophy that excludes God. But the drive to understand leads eventually to what theologian Paul Tillich called "the riddle of all riddles—the mystery that there is anything at all."

We are so accustomed to taking for granted that the universe exists, it startles us to think it might have been otherwise. But if you ponder the matter for a moment, you will see that there is no *necessary* reason for the existence of the world.

Atheism cannot provide any clue to the riddle of why there is something instead of nothing. Theism answers the riddle by saying, "In the beginning, God. . . ." "That which does not exist begins to exist only through something already existing," said the great scholastic Thomas Aquinas. Therefore the chain of causation must lead ultimately to something whose existence is not contingent but necessary. The riddle of existence ultimately can be solved only by postulating a self-existent Creator, an Uncaused First Cause.

You may find it as hard to conceive of a self-existent God as to conceive of a self-existent universe. If so, begin instead with a fact on which everyone can agree: for some reason, the universe *is* here. Through science and observation, man has learned a good bit about it. The question is which hypothesis—atheism or theism—is more compatible with the observed phenomena.

The assumption that science has invalidated belief in God is very widely held today as a result of the mind-setting attitudes of contemporary culture which we discussed previously. But it is repudiated by many prominent scientists.

Professor Claud Tresmontant, a distinguished French scientist, says just the opposite is true. The discoveries of modern science have made it clear that the universe is evolving in a direction impossible to explain without recourse to the hypothesis that there is a creative mind and purpose behind it.

It is theoretically possible, he says, that blind chance is the sole causative force at work in the universe. But in light of contemporary knowledge "it is so extremely improbable that only a few scientists now seriously think that pure chance can explain the universe."

"For matter to have been able on its own to invent biological evolution, which has constantly tended through the ages toward the creation of ever more complex and differentiated organisms, endowed with bigger brains and an ever greater degree of consciousness, it must be gifted with great wisdom and incomparable genius," says the French scholar. "Indeed, matter must be credited with all the attributes that theologians specify as belonging to God."

Pierre Teilhard de Chardin, the great French paleontologist-priest who devoted his life to working out a synthesis of scientific and religious thought, also found in the facts of evolution irresistible testimony to the operation of a divine purpose.

If we had to reckon only with mindless matter, Teilhard says, we should expect it to obey the second law of thermodynamics, which affirms a universal trend toward the equal distribution of energy throughout all space. The logical result of the unchecked operation of this law would be a gradual decay of all complex organisms toward simpler and less differentiated states.

But what we actually observe in the universe is exactly the reverse: a process of "complexification," going on for billions of years, moving from inanimate matter to living organisms, evolving ever higher forms of life, and finally bringing forth the supremely improbable phenomenon of man, a creature endowed with the capacity for self-consciousness, reflective thought, and the exercise of will.

But it is not only the upward direction of evolution that defies explanation by the laws of probability, Teilhard says. It is equally impossible to account, within a purely materialistic world view, for the basic hospitality of the natural environment toward life. This is a world in which life has been able to emerge, flourish, and persist, and it is very hard to believe that such a world could just happen. Those who have more than a speaking acquaintance with the life sciences find their minds reeling, Teilhard says, when they "try to number the favourable circumstances which must coincide at every moment if the least of living things is to survive and to succeed in its enterprises."

The evidence of design which science finds in the natural universe is particularly striking when we consider the achieve-

THE IMPACT OF MODERN SCIENCE ON BELIEF

ment of evolution which would be most improbable if the world were the product of blind chance. In the very act of reading this sentence, you are demonstrating that achievement, which is a capacity for *thought*.

"The emergence of even the simplest mind from no mind at all seems, to me at least, utterly incomprehensible," says biologist Sewall Wright.

Still another intimation of the reality of God is the sense of absolute obligation which all of us sometimes experience. Efforts have been made to explain man's moral consciousness as a survival of ancient taboos and rules laid down for the preservation of society. But this pat explanation simply will not cover the case of the individual who chooses to oppose the society that surrounds him even though his opposition will be costly. Socrates drinking hemlock, Christ dying on the cross, an American youth going to jail rather than to war refute any attempt to equate morality with social conformity.

Another distinctive human attribute which seems to intimate that there is more to the world than dumb matter and blind chance is our capacity to appreciate beauty—not only the beauty that is created by human effort, such as music and art, but also and especially that which we find in nature.

Chance collisions of atoms might produce a certain amount of accidental beauty in a universe that consisted solely of mindless matter. But persistent and abundant beauty, unnecessary beauty that has no practical function, beauty that speaks to the part of man which lies deeper than words or conscious thoughts can penetrate—does not this suggest there may be, behind natural processes, an Artist who creates beauty for its own sake?

I do not contend that these rational arguments constitute irrefutable logical "proof" of the reality of God. But I do think any open-minded person must acknowledge that the evidence *for* God, on a purely scientific and rational basis, is very strong indeed.

★ Questions to ponder or discuss

Can you think of any specific discovery of modern science that has invalidated belief in God?

Can you think of any way of explaining the evolutionary process that does *not* in some way attribute design and purposiveness to nature?

Do you know any other purely rational arguments for the existence of God?

4 ✹ *Caricatures of God*

A mother once found her five-year-old daughter busily engaged with crayon and paper.

"What are you drawing, dear?" she inquired.

"I'm drawing a picture of God," said the little girl.

"But no one knows what God looks like," objected mother, seizing eagerly upon what she took to be a teachable moment.

"They will when I'm through," replied the young artist.

Unfortunately, five-year-old girls are not the only people who are serenely confident of their ability to depict God. Theologians through the centuries have defined the nature of God with a degree of dogmatism from which a modest naturalist would shrink in describing a beetle.

Undertaking to delineate the nature and attributes of God is not only brash; it is inevitably misleading. "Make any truth too definite and you make it too small," said Samuel Taylor Coleridge, and the warning applies particularly to theology. Any concept of deity that is within the grasp of finite human minds—however brilliant—is bound to limit, and therefore distort, the infinite and incomprehensible reality which men have in mind when they utter the word "God."

25

If all conceptions of God are inadequate, does it really matter which ones we have? Yes, it does. Experience has shown that some images and analogies do *point toward* God, even though they fail to encompass him. And it also has demonstrated that other conceptions are so inadequate as to be misleading and harmful.

One misleading concept of God, which is very widely held today, is reflected in the time-honored custom of referring to God as "the Supreme Being."

As the late Paul Tillich pointed out, this phrase inevitably suggests that God is a particular entity (being) who exists at some particular spatial location. And this is of course nonsense. Jewish and Christian theologians have maintained for thousands of years that God is *not* "up there" or "out there" or indeed any*where,* because his reality transcends the space-time continuum within which mere created entities exist.

To steer our minds away from space-bound anthropomorphic images, Tillich said that God is not a being at all, but rather is "the Ground of Being, . . . the reason why anything at all exists."

The custom of referring to God as a person also tends to arouse anthropomorphic images which are stumbling blocks to mature faith. When people are asked to believe in "a personal God," they immediately start thinking in terms of a very big man. The difficulty is compounded when they go on to fill in details of the *kind* of extra-large man they think God is.

Two images seem to dominate popular imagination. One is that of the Great Scorekeeper in the Sky, a harsh, unloving, and unlovable fellow who lays down strict rules knowing his human creatures cannot keep them, and gleefully marks up each transgression, awaiting the day when he can subject them to brutal and unremitting punishment.

This concept is highly uncomplimentary to God and is directly contradictory to everything that Jesus Christ taught

26

about the loving, forgiving, accepting, ever-merciful nature of God.

At the opposite pole is the image of God as our Grandfather in Heaven. This conception has acquired a tremendous following in modern America. It comforts people who are enjoying the benefits of an affluent society and would like to believe that their luxuries are the just reward of their virtues and a token of God's complete satisfaction with their way of life. But this view of God does not come from the Bible. It tells over and over again of good men who suffered for serving God, and of wicked men who prospered. In the New Testament, we find Jesus using the image of a loving father to convey a sense of God's disposition toward human creatures. But in the Jewish homes of first-century Palestine, the father was not an ineffectual, overindulgent soft touch. He was the benevolent but undisputed ruler of the household, and he was far more concerned with the spiritual welfare and growth of his children than with insuring them instant access to every creature comfort they might desire.

If the concept of a "personal God" leads to such aberrations, *deviation from the right path* should we abandon it and speak of God solely in abstract terms such as "Ground of Being" or "Ultimate Reality"?

I think that would be even more misleading. Personality is the highest and most complex category of reality we have discovered in the universe. We must assume that God's reality infinitely transcends human personality, but we certainly have no warrant for thinking that it can be expressed in any lesser category.

To speak of God as "he" may be inadequate and confusing. But to speak of God as "it" is insulting.

Moreover, as the Canadian theologian Leslie Dewart has pointed out, "God's relations with man are necessarily personal, for *we* are persons." A flower or a stone or a star may experience God as an impersonal force, but men experience God as "thou."

★ Questions to ponder or discuss

Do you know anyone who has rejected belief in God because the only concept of deity he has ever encountered is one to which no intelligent adult could give credence?

Is there any concept or image of God which you picked up in childhood that has been a stumbling block for you personally?

How would you describe God to a child? To an educated adult?

5 ☀ The Problem of Evil

Atheism's strongest case against God is summarized in this assertion:

If there were a God, infinite in power and love, he would have created a perfect world. All of his creatures would be happy. They would not bring misery upon themselves through moral evils such as war and racial hatred. They would not suffer from dreadful diseases such as cancer. They would not be at the mercy of natural disasters such as earthquakes and floods.

Since evil, pain, and trouble are abundantly manifest in this world, the atheist concludes, it cannot be the work of an all-wise, all-powerful, all-loving Creator. It can only be regarded as a product of blind chance, a working-out of impersonal material forces which are indifferent to the happiness of such sentient creatures as may evolve within their midst.

This argument sounds extremely plausible. In fact, when you first encounter it, you may think it unanswerable.

But it isn't quite as formidable as it seems. It contains two great fallacies.

The first is its implicit assumption that the only purpose a loving God could possibly have is to place his human creatures in a pleasure-filled paradise where all they have to do is enjoy themselves.

John Hick, a Cambridge University philosopher, comments on this assumption in his book *Evil and the God of Love:*

"Those who use the problem of evil as an argument against belief in God almost invariably think of God's relation to the world on the model of a human being building a cage for a pet animal. If he is humane, he will naturally make his pet's quarters as pleasant and healthful as he can. Any respect in which the cage falls short of the veterinarian's ideal, and contains possibilities of accident or disease, is evidence of either limited benevolence or limited means, or both."

But this view completely misreads God's purpose and his attitude toward humanity, Hick says.

"Men are not to be thought of on the analogy of animal pets, whose life is to be made as agreeable as possible, but rather on the analogy of human children, who are to grow to adulthood in an environment whose primary and overriding purpose is not immediate pleasure but the realizing of the most valuable potentialities of human personality.

"This world was not intended to be a paradise; . . . it is a place of soul-making."

Must "soul-making" be accompanied by so much travail? Couldn't an omnipotent God have created men who were spiritually perfect to begin with?

Theoretically, yes. But the automatic goodness of ready-made saints evidently is less precious to God than the flawed and sweaty goodness achieved by fallible men through struggling with temptations and making responsible choices in difficult situations.

We need not suppose that every ill which befalls an individual or a nation is "sent" by God as a punishment, a corrective, or a challenge. What God has created is a stable universe governed by natural laws—a universe in which the rain falls upon the just and the unjust alike, and in which a cancer cell is as likely to invade the body of a saint as that of a sinner.

Capricious disasters and undeserved suffering contribute to the soul-making process because they call forth the noblest of all human responses. Men and women often act with unselfish generosity and kindness when they see others afflicted with unmerited misery. It's hard to see how courage could emerge except in a world inhabited by danger, or how compassion could be called forth without the reality of pain.

To regard this world as a crucible in which souls are forged makes sense, of course, only if we take seriously the Christian assurance that death is not the end of the human adventure.

Cynics may dismiss this as "pie in the sky when you die." But there is no other basis on which the manifest wrongs and injustices of this life can be fitted into any philosophy which ascribes purpose to creation and meaning to human existence.

The "problem of evil" really confronts us not with a riddle but with a choice. We can reject the idea of another state of existence after death—in which case we must abandon our attempt to reconcile the kind of world we have with the concept of a loving God. Or we can affirm the Christian hope of eternal life—and believe with St. Paul that the sufferings of this present time are not worthy to be compared with the glory that shall be revealed in us as the children of God.

★ Questions to ponder or discuss

If you had a choice, would you rather be treated as a pet-in-a-playpen or as a son growing up under the tutelage of a father who loves you too much to spoil you with soft indulgence?

Why do you believe (or disbelieve, as the case may be) in life after death?

6 ☀ Is God Omnipotent?

In the preceding section, I said there are two great fallacies in the seemingly plausible argument that the existence of evil proves the world cannot be the work of a loving God. The first fallacy, which we've already considered, is the assumption that God's purpose was to create a hedonistic paradise.

The second fallacy stems from the widely held idea that God is omnipotent, or all-powerful.

To most people, omnipotence means that God can do anything he wants and there is no real power other than that of God. In other words, God is thought of as an Oriental sultan, whose domain is universal and whose reign is eternal. He is therefore responsible for everything that happens in the world, just as it happens.

This concept of God's omnipotence completely ignores what science tells us, and our own experience confirms, about the radical freedom that exists in the universe, at every level from the random movement of electrons to the darting thoughts of a human mind.

Some of our best contemporary theologians, building on the thought of the great British scientist-philosopher Alfred North Whitehead, have learned to avoid the logical trap inherent in the doctrine of omnipotence by speaking of creation not as a finished product but as a *process*. God ordained the process, they say, and he is continually active in it. But he does not have a monopoly of power, and his will is not the only factor operative within the process. He certainly could have had a monopoly of power had he seen fit, but he evidently values freedom so highly that he chose to endow his creation with it even though this decision inevitably opens the way to capricious accident and deliberate evil.

John B. Cobb, Jr., one of the most articulate of the "process theologians," points out that the notion of God's having a monopoly of power is entirely foreign to the Bible, which depicts God as being engaged in a constant struggle to maximize the good and minimize the evil in a world in which his will can be, and quite often is, defied.

Moreover, says Cobb, the doctrine of omnipotence attributes the wrong kind of power to God. It assumes that God's power is "the power to compel or force." And this is "a wretched and pitiful form of power" which even a human parent should disdain to use in dealing with his children, except as a last resort.

The New Testament offers a clue to the real nature of God's power. It is the kind of power exercised by a wise and effective parent—the power of persuasion.

"The only power capable of any worthwhile result is the power of persuasion," Cobb argues. "If we think of God's power as persuasive power, we may still use the term omnipotence if we like, but its meaning is quite altered. It no longer means that God exercises a monopoly of power and compels everything to be just as it is. It means instead that he exercises some optimum of persuasive power in relation to whatever is. Such an optimum is a balance between urging toward the good and maximizing the power—and therefore the freedom—of the one whom God seeks to persuade."

Another process theologian, Norman Pittenger, says the traditional view of divine omnipotence assumes that God is in every respect absolute, and determines in precise detail everything that happens.

"But such a God is only an idol, modeled on man's worst image of himself; for we regard as utterly despicable a man who dictates everything that his family and friends shall do," says Pittenger.

"A much better model would be the man whose character is sheer goodness, who is always faithful to his purpose and loyal to his friends, who 'lets them be' but is affected by what they think and do, and who yet has enough resources of love to adapt himself to new circumstances and situations, and to make the best that can conceivably be made of them.

"That, I suggest, is the sort of model which makes sense of God in the world we live in. It is a world in which there is chance, there is risk, there is recalcitrance. Yet goodness is known, truth is obtainable, beauty is present within that world—and above all, love is experienced there."

The pain and evil of the world are comprehensible if we recognize that God has chosen to be a father, not a dictator; a fellow sufferer, not a tyrant.

But—and this point is invariably overlooked by those who glibly cite "the problem of evil" as a refutation of belief in God—the beauty, truth, and goodness which we encounter and experience would be quite inexplicable if the world were the mindless product of blind chance.

★ Questions to ponder or discuss

Was God right to leave room in the universe for freedom, spontaneity, and a degree of self-determination on the part of his creatures? Or would you have done things differently?

Can you conceive of any way in which God could have permitted freedom without also permitting the possibility that accidental or intentional harm would be inflicted upon his creatures?

7 ☀ Who Needs God?

What practical difference does it make to us, here and now, whether God is real or just a figment of human imagination?

Well, in the first place, what we believe about God has a profound effect on how we act—on the practical choices and decisions we make every day in our lives.

If God is a delusion, there is no compelling reason why I should put the welfare of others or the best interests of my community and my country above my own narrow self-interest.

You may challenge that statement by pointing to atheists who live highly moral lives, who make noble sacrifices in the service of mankind. I know people like that and admire them. But I think they are living on inherited capital. They continue to live by certain values derived from our Christian heritage, because they have found them good and true, even though they no longer subscribe to the religious concepts which are the ultimate sanctions of those values.

But people who are able to continue living by Christian values, after repudiating the theological beliefs behind those values, seem to be a rapidly diminishing minority in this country. All around us today we see depressing evidence that a very large number of people no longer feel bound by any higher law than what they can get away with.

This decay of the moral sense which obliges men to behave in certain ways, whether or not it is to their immediate advantage, is one of the root causes of the strife and disunity and dislocation that presently poison our national life.

In the fall of 1969, a group of forty Nobel Prize winners—including some of the world's most eminent physical and social scientists—assembled in Stockholm for a five-day symposium on "The Place of Value in a World of Facts." It was their consensus that civilization is gravely imperiled by the loss of axiomatic, transcendent values.

Writer Arthur Koestler bluntly accused physical scientists of bringing about the crisis by treating man as though he were "nothing but a complex biochemical mechanism."

"Keep telling a man that he is nothing but an oversized rat, and he will grow whiskers and bite your fingers," Koestler warned.

Another Nobel laureate, Harvard biologist George Wald, put it even more strongly: "The only way the world is going to stop short of the brink of nuclear holocaust is a return to God."

Dr. Wald conceded that it may sound like "the sheerest non-academic sentimentality" to say that faith, hope, and love are not merely desirable, but indispensable to human survival. "But I'm convinced that this is the only way we are going to prevent the total chaos we're headed for."

An observant newspaperman, Anthony Lewis of the *New York Times,* has sought to explain why the whole fabric of society is jeopardized, particularly in America, by the widespread loss of belief in God.

"It is not just the fact of poverty and physical ugliness in the richest of all countries that troubles us; these are problems that our technical apparatus could solve. What we lack is any agreed moral basis of their solution. . . .

"Today no shared vision elevates the spirit of Americans, or for that matter of Frenchmen or Italians or Britons. The dominant mood of selfishness is met by strains of anarchy. There are dedicated individuals, but the mass imagination is not stirred to acts of nobility or sacrifice.

"It is not a question of ideology. The Communist experiment began with that, and the result is a system that rigidly excludes the humane. What we miss is something vaguer, a broad area of shared belief in something nobler than physical satisfactions. Without it we lack confidence in the future of our own societies; we grow surly."

Beyond all considerations of moral conduct and social order, what a person believes about God also has a profound effect on his capacity for *happiness*.

I do not mean to imply that if you believe in God, everything will come up roses for you. The notion that faith is some sort of insurance policy against hardship and suffering is forever belied by the example of our Lord Jesus Christ. His faith in God was complete, but it did not render him immune to pain and death. And he made it very clear that we who would follow him can also expect to encounter, in this world, trouble and travail.

But all men have troubles—whether they believe in God or not. The great difference is that if we believe in God, we can *accept* a world in which we find both pain and pleasure, good and evil, joy and sadness, without falling into the despairing conclusion that life is meaningless and absurd.

In his autobiography, Bertrand Russell speaks of "that terrible loneliness in which one shivering consciousness looks over the rim of the world into the cold unfathomable lifeless abyss." Russell said it was this feeling of perpetual loneliness that made him so desperately eager to establish and maintain close human relationships:

"What else is there to make life tolerable on the shore of an ocean, crying to the emptiness? . . . The world seems to me

37

quite dreadful; the unhappiness of most people is very great, and I often wonder how they will endure it. I suppose if they did not live most of the time in the things of the moment, they would not be able to go on."

By liberating us from this oppressive sense of ultimate futility, belief in God makes it possible to be happy even in the midst of trials and tribulations. And again, I will point to Jesus as an example. The Jesus whom we encounter in the Gospels radiates a contagious joy, bubbling up from well-springs of the spirit too deep to be contaminated by the external vicissitudes of life.

Whatit comes down to is this: If God exists, then life does have a purpose—it does make sense—it is leading *somewhere,* even though I may not at the moment be able to discern exactly where or why. If God does not exist, then the whole thing is a bad joke—*on us.* The first hypothesis leads to peace; the second leads to despair.

★ Questions to ponder or discuss

If the decision were left entirely up to you, would you decree that God be real or nonexistent? Why?

If you want to believe in God, do you find that this very fact arouses in you a secret fear that your faith in him may be based upon wishful thinking? Is this really a valid fear or does it merely reflect the degree to which you've been conditioned by the prevailing assumptions of a hyperskeptical culture?

8 ⚜ Stones and Bread

We've been inundated in recent years with books, articles, and even in some churches sermons proclaiming that it has become impossible for "modern man" to believe in an order of reality transcending nature.

If the church is to gain a hearing from "modern man," we have been told, it must forthwith purge its teachings of all talk about miracles or supernatural events. The Bible must be "demythologized" and the resurrection must be presented as a psychological happening in the minds and hearts of the disciples.

That's what we've been told by the radical theologians who've dominated the idea market in recent years.

However, we have *not* been told—at least, no one has managed to make clear to me—*why* we must jettison about 90 percent of the historic Christian faith. We have simply been told, in a more dogmatic tone than any Roman pope has dared to employ for some time, that this is the way it *has* to be if we want to communicate with "modern man."

Now I cannot speak with the same assurance as the radical theologians do about the mind-set of "modern man." To be perfectly honest, I must confess that in thirty years as a newspaper reporter, I've never met the fellow. He seems to be as elusive in real life as that "common man" Henry Wallace used to talk about.

In my quest for the prototype "modern man" I *have* met and talked to a good many individual modern men. I've even listened to some of them. And what I hear these modern men saying is that they're sick and tired of being told what they *can't* believe. They want to know what, if anything, they *can* believe.

They feel they've been cast long enough in the role of captive audience for theologians engaged in a reckless competition to see who can administer the rudest shock to the faithful.

Most of them aren't particularly interested in the denatured Christianity which is being offered to them as a concession to their supposed modernity of mind. They figure that if the church is just a human institution for social service, if the Bible is so unreliable that you can't take any part of it very seriously, if the Christian faith is based on a gigantic lie about a man rising from the dead—then there's no use trying to "modernize" this mess. Just throw it all out and be done with it.

This growing disenchantment among the laity is, I believe, the main reason why we are witnessing a decline in church attendance and a relative decline in giving. Some religious leaders like to attribute these trends to lay disapproval of church social action. This explanation strikes me as rather self-righteous. It says, in effect, "We are suffering because we, like Christ, have stood up for the right."

My own observation is otherwise. For every layman I know who has quit coming to church because he disapproves of social action, I know at least three who are hanging on and supporting the church only because it *is* a channel for community service.

The real lesson to be drawn from the slump in religious interest seems to me quite clear. If you persist in handing out stones when people ask for bread, they'll finally quit coming to the bakery.

Happily, there are signs that we are approaching the end of the fad for reckless negation in theology. Authors of impressive scholarly standing finally have come forward to assure bewildered laymen that "modern man" *can* believe in God—even in a personal, loving, purposeful God—without the slightest sacrifice of intellectual integrity.

Indeed, some have gone so far as to argue—quite cogently, it seems to me—that "modern man" really can't make sense of all the phenomena of his own existence without the hypothesis of God.

Over in Europe, whence we belatedly imported demythologizing, a new generation of theologians has arisen who are treating the resurrection as an actual, historical event.

And now comes that handsomely credentialed liberal, Peter Berger, to rehabilitate the term "supernatural." Miracles, obviously, have not ceased.

Dr. Berger, a sociologist, says in his book *A Rumor of Angels:*

"It may be conceded that there is in the modern world a certain type of consciousness that has difficulties with the supernatural. This statement remains, however, on the level of sociohistorical diagnosis. The diagnosed condition is *not* thereupon elevated to the status of absolute criterion. . . . We may agree that contemporary consciousness is incapable of conceiving of either angels or demons. We are still left with the question of whether, possibly, both angels and demons go on existing despite this incapacity of our contemporaries to conceive of them."

I am not greatly exercised, personally, about the existence of angels and demons. But I must confess that I am heartened to find myself in a changing theological climate which makes it possible to admit that I say the Lord's Prayer without crossing my fingers.

★ Questions to ponder or discuss

Has your faith in God been shaken by the radical theologians?

Which viewpoint has been most disturbing to you? Why?

Is it wise to rest your faith on any secondhand "authority" or indeed on anything other than your own *experience* of the reality of God?

9 ✺ *Behold the Man!*

What was he really like, this Jesus of Nazareth whom the church claims as its founder?

Although his name is familiar to nearly everyone—so familiar it has become a casual expletive—the man himself remains, for many, a shadowy figure.

Even those who worship him as Lord and Savior are in perpetual danger of forgetting that Jesus—whatever else he may have been—was fully and authentically human.

From the earliest days of the church until now, there has been a tendency among pious folk to feel that it is somehow a little blasphemous to speak of Jesus as a man who got tired and sweaty, hungry and discouraged, lonely and frightened, even as other men do.

But the slighting of Jesus' humanity is not piety: it is heresy, and has been so labeled by the church since the Council of Chalcedon in A.D. 451.

One thing we can say positively about the man Jesus is that he was a real person who lived and taught and died in Palestine about 2,000 years ago. Every now and then, someone comes up with the notion that Jesus was a purely mythical figure, like Hercules or Beowulf. But this won't wash. There are references to Jesus not only in Christian literature but also in Roman and Jewish histories. "No reputable historian today doubts the existence of Jesus," says Dr. John Knox.

The New Testament Gospels, which are our main source of information about Jesus, are not full-length biographies. They are more like magazine profiles. They give us a vivid picture of Jesus, largely through a succession of anecdotes, but they do not contain a great amount of connected narrative. And they omit many details which a modern biographer would include as a matter of course.

For example, none of the Gospels gives a physical description of Jesus. The thousands of "portraits" of Jesus which have been painted through the centuries are based entirely on inference and artistic imagination.

It can be inferred, with confidence, that Jesus was a tall man—because Gospel anecdotes reveal he was easily spotted in crowds. It also is virtually certain that he wore long hair and a beard, as nearly all male Jews did in his day.

We know much more about his personality than we do about his appearance. The Gospels make clear that he was capable of both great toughness and great tenderness. He was courageous in his confrontations with the rich and the mighty, compassionate in his dealings with the poor and the weak. No matter how weary or harassed he was, he never retired into a shell of self-concern. He always cared.

Although his sensitivity to the needs of others made him share the misery of every suffering person he encountered, he was not essentially a sad person. On the contrary, he radiated a contagious happiness—a sense of the sheer joy of living.

Some people have gotten the notion—perhaps from our Puritan forebears—that Jesus was a dour ascetic who disdained such normal human pleasures as social activities. But the Gospels report just the opposite. Jesus loved a good party —and was a much sought-after dinner guest. His appreciation of good food and good wine was so evident that the strait-

44

laced Pharisees scornfully referred to him as "a glutton and winebibber."

But pleasure was never a major preoccupation of Jesus' life. He was too deeply concerned about the welfare of others to give much thought to his own comfort. In the phrase which the modern police blotter reserves for vagrants, he had "no fixed address" and no regular income. He accepted such hospitality as was offered him during his itinerant ministry, and was perfectly willing, when necessary, to go without supper and sleep in the open fields.

Perhaps the worst insult which people unintentionally direct at Jesus is to think of him as "meek and mild."

Actually, he was just the opposite. He was a bold and outspoken man who rebelled against convention and trampled heavily on the tenderest corns of the Establishment.

If you define "radical" with Webster's dictionary as "one who favors fundamental or extreme change," then Jesus was the greatest radical of all time.

Other revolutionaries have sought only to shake up political and economic systems. Jesus turned upside down the whole value system by which the world lives.

He said it is better to give than to receive, better to love than to be loved, better to suffer wrongs than to seek revenge, better to be poor and humble than to be rich and proud, better to die trusting in the ultimate vindication of God's righteousness than to live with a craven compromise.

Jesus can be worshiped, loved, admired, rejected, or hated. But he cannot easily be ignored. After twenty centuries, his radically unselfish life style remains a challenge to which each of us sooner or later must respond in some way.

★ Questions to ponder or discuss

Salvador Dali's famous painting of the Last Supper, which hangs in the National Gallery of Art in Washington, D.C., shows Jesus with his arms outstretched so that hair is plainly visible in his armpits. Do you find this detail shocking or offensive?

If so, what does this reaction say about your attitude toward the humanity of Jesus?

10 ☀ *Why the Bells Ring at Christmas*

The shepherds were frightened when the angel appeared. But the angel said: "Don't be afraid. For I am here with good news for you, which will bring joy to all the people."

The coming of Christ is "good news"—for you, for me, for all people. That was the herald angel's proclamation on the first Christmas Eve. It is still the basic rationale of Christmas festivity.

Nearly everyone would agree, probably, that the birth of Christ is "good news" in the sense that the world has been a better place because of his life and teaching.

But the herald angel meant a great deal more than that. And it is the more that makes Christmas an occasion for joyous celebration by all men in all ages.

What the angel meant—and what has always been the heart of the Christian gospel—is that Christ was the living embodiment of a message which God was unable to get across to mankind in any other way.

The message is simple and enormously comforting.

God does not hate us. He loves us.

He does not wish to punish us for our errant ways. He seeks reconciliation and offers forgiveness.

The destiny he has prepared for us is not extinction, which would render our brief existence ultimately meaningless. He offers us eternal communion with his own timeless being, and thereby confers crucial importance on each deed and word and thought by which we become more or less worthy to be called his sons.

The distinguished British theologian Erik Routley points out that men have an ingrained tendency to suspect that God is hostile toward them.

This is a hangover from the primitive era of religion when gods were thought to be vengeful and capricious beings who had to be appeased by every means possible. Some versions of Christian theology have helped to perpetuate this unflattering concept of God, Routley says, by depicting Christ as a scapegoat who sacrificed himself in order to assuage God's hatred of humanity.

But this, says Routley, is "a pernicious distortion of the truth."

"Jesus Christ did not come to stand for us over against God: to vindicate mankind against a God who disbelieved in man's worthiness to be saved. The office of Christ was not to represent men to God, but to be God among men. Where men were saying constantly that 'God must be caused to love the world,' Christ said, 'God is Love'—meaning that God loves the world and has always loved it."

That is indeed good news, forever relevant, perennially fresh, worthy of being celebrated with joy over and over again.

★ Questions to ponder or discuss

St. Paul said in a famous passage of one of his letters, "God was in Christ, reconciling the world unto himself." What does this statement mean *to you?*

There are some widely held theories of the atonement which

make God seem like a ruthless judge whose wrath against "sinners" could be appeased only by the spilling of innocent blood. Have you encountered such a doctrine? Were you put off by it? Do you realize that the church has never accepted any specific theory or explanation of the atonement as a final answer to be enshrined in dogma?

11 ☀ *It Happened on Friday*

It had been a long night, and he was already exhausted when they brought him before the Roman governor for trial.

He had been betrayed by one of his disciples and deserted by the others. There had been a rowdy preliminary hearing during which his captors slapped him around and shouted at him.

Now, through the haze of fatigue, he heard Pontius Pilate pronouncing the most dreaded sentence a Roman court could impose:

"Crucify him."

Imperial Rome was not noted for its gentleness with condemned men. But even the Romans had qualms about this horrible method of execution which they had learned from the Persians. No Roman citizen could be put to death by crucifixion, whatever his crime. It was reserved for slaves and fomenters of revolutions.

Roman soldiers seized him roughly and hustled him off to their barracks. These soldiers were members of the second Roman cohort, stationed in Palestine on occupation duty. They feared and hated the proud people whom they kept in subjugation. Now they had a chance to vent their anti-semitism on one who had been found guilty of claiming to be "the King of the Jews."

They bound him by the wrists to a post in the outdoor court of the barracks and took turns lashing his bare back with a whip. It was a special kind of whip called a scourge, made of leather straps weighted with bits of metal.

Prisoners often died from a scourging. But the soldiers planned a little horseplay with this one. So they quit flogging him while he was still conscious.

One barracks wit took off his scarlet legionnaire's cloak and put it over the prisoner's shoulders, in imitation of a king's royal purple robe. Another plaited a crown of sharp briars to fit on his head. Someone else put a reed in his hand to resemble a scepter. Then they approached his "throne" one by one, kneeling before him in mock homage, and arising to spit in his face.

About 8:00 A.M., they led him out to crucify him.

It was customary to make a prisoner carry his own cross to the place of execution. But the terrible beating he had received had left him almost too weak to walk, and so the soldiers seized a passerby named Simon and compelled him to carry the cross. Simon was from Cyrene, a city in North Africa. Ancient tradition holds that he was a Negro.

The execution site was known as "Golgotha" (in Latin, Calvary), which means "place of a skull." It was on a hill outside the city walls, near one of the main roads into Jerusalem.

They stripped off all of his clothing. It was part of the humiliation of crucifixion that the prisoner should hang there naked. His clothing became the property of the execution squad. They divided some of his garments among them, and cast dice for a seamless tunic which could not be divided.

Now came the worst part. They set him astride a wooden peg which jutted out from the upright pole of the cross, and

51

made him stretch out his arms along the crossbeam. They drove nails through the palms of his hands to hold him there.

Then they nailed his feet to the upright pole, in an awkward position that insured the utmost agony to the muscles of his limp and hanging body.

Some pious women of Jerusalem made a practice of going to crucifixions and administering a heavily drugged wine to condemned men to alleviate their suffering. The good women were on hand today. But this prisoner refused their opiate.

It was 9:00 o'clock in the morning when they nailed him to the cross. It usually took about twelve hours for a crucified man to die from the shock of excruciating pain. The Roman author Cicero records that many of the victims became raving madmen. It was often necessary to cut out their tongues to put a stop to their terrible screams and curses.

But this was a most unusual person. As he looked down from the cross at the people who were laughing and sneering at his helpless plight, he was heard to say: "Father, forgive them, for they know not what they do."

Weakened by the scourging, he did not take long to die. Only six hours.

Toward the end, he cried aloud: "My God, my God, why hast thou forsaken me?"

Commentators have been pointing out ever since that these are the opening words of the twenty-second psalm, which devout Jews used as a prayer in extremity. But no amount of scholarly explanation can minimize the sheer human agony of mind and spirit reflected in that pathetic cry.

Even in his final hour, however, he did not become pre-occupied with his own troubles. He was still concerned about others. He saw his mother weeping at the foot of the cross, and asked a friend to take her home. He spoke words of comfort to another condemned man undergoing the same torture.

At 3:00 P.M. he said: "Father, into thy hands I commit my spirit."

It was finished. His Father would take care of the rest.

★ Questions to ponder or discuss

Was it really necessary for Jesus to die on a cross? Suppose he had modified his message a bit, and made enough compromises to keep the Establishment from regarding him as a dangerous subversive. Would that have affected his mission— or the impact of his life on all subsequent history?

If you were a Roman official or a Jewish religious leader in the first century A.D., and a man came along who seemed to be stirring up the common people with radical ideas, would *you* feel he had to be dealt with severely?

Were the men who crucified Jesus Jews . . . or Romans . . . or simply representatives of the human race doing what comes all too naturally to all of us?

12 ☀ And Did He Really Rise?

The Christian faith was founded on the unqualified assertion that Jesus Christ returned to life after being crucified, dead, and buried.

There are three ways of looking at this claim.

First, it can be regarded as a gigantic hoax. Followers of Jesus may have proclaimed his resurrection after secretly removing his corpse from its burial place.

This view has appealed to many, from the first century A.D. to the present. According to Matthew's Gospel, it was the official explanation put out by the authorities in Jerusalem after Jesus' tomb was found empty. Its enduring popularity is attested by its reappearance in a recent best seller, *The Passover Plot*.

A second possibility is that the resurrection was a purely subjective experience of the early Christian community.

According to this view, Jesus remained physically dead but came to life again in the minds and hearts of his disciples. Thus Easter was not an event in the life of Jesus, but an event in the lives of the disciples.

Many theological liberals subscribe to this interpretation.

The third possibility is that it really happened as the Bible says: Three days after his death, the crucified Christ appeared, alive and tangible, to his disciples.

It is not easy to believe in the resurrection as an objective historical event. The massive weight of ordinary human experience testifies that dead men stay dead. It should be remembered, however, that this fact was as well known in the first century as it is today.

The disciples certainly did not expect to see Jesus again. Their dumbfounded surprise is clearly reflected in the gospel records. Even after a group of women returned with breathless news of the empty tomb, Luke's Gospel records that the male disciples "thought that what the women said was nonsense, and did not believe them."

What changed their minds? The answer is given by the apostle Paul in one of the oldest Christian documents known, the First Letter to the Corinthians:

"I passed on to you what I received, which is of the greatest importance: That Christ died for our sins, as written in the Scriptures; that he was buried and raised to life on the third day, as written in the Scriptures; that he appeared to Peter, and then to all twelve apostles. Then he appeared to more than five hundred of his followers at once, most of whom are still alive."

The disciples believed in the resurrection not because they found it plausible that a dead man should live again, but because they saw, heard, talked to, and touched the risen Christ. Confronted with the overwhelming reality of his presence, they no longer asked whether such a thing was credible.

Were they victims of mass hallucination? Possibly. But to anyone who has read their records, and has seen what plain, down-to-earth, unimaginative, basically skeptical fishermen and peasants they were, this hypothesis is very hard to sustain.

Was it purely a subjective spiritual experience of the disciples? If it was no more than that, one wonders why the disciples' enemies, who were numerous, did not promptly cut the ground from under the story by producing the remains of Jesus. The rapid growth of the Christian church in a hostile environment strongly indicates that its enemies did not have available the sure and easy refutation of its gospel which would have been provided by a body in the tomb.

Did they make it up? That explanation seems even more improbable than mass hallucination when you consider that the disciples suffered martyrdom in droves rather than change their story. Men do not cheerfully lay down their lives to perpetuate a hoax.

Did it really happen? The question must be answered ultimately by each individual for himself. The only verification available at this time is that which comes through the kind of personal experience which follows upon, and is part of, the adventure of faith.

The Christian church is composed, at its core, of men and women who are convinced they have encountered Jesus Christ as a real and living presence. It is out of their own experience, as well as in reliance on the New Testament record, that they join in proclaiming:

"He IS risen!"

★ Questions to ponder or discuss

What is your theory about the resurrection? Do you regard it as a hoax, a purely subjective event in the minds and hearts of the disciples, or a real event? What reasoning or experience has led you to this conclusion?

Markus Barth has said: "The arguments proffered to disprove the historicity of the resurrection are at least as dogmatically prejudiced and fallible as the arguments to the contrary." What does he mean by this? Do you agree?

13 ☀ A Presence and a Power

In their effort to communicate with modern man, Christian theologians are returning to the language of the early church.

They're talking more and more about the Holy Spirit.

And they are discovering that contemporary minds are quite receptive to the original biblical concept of the Holy Spirit as God-in-action in the everyday world.

The apostle Paul and other authors of the New Testament had a great deal to say about the Holy Spirit. But they were concerned primarily with the Spirit's activity. It was so real to them that they felt no need of definitions and explanations.

It wasn't until the third and fourth centuries A.D. that church fathers began to embalm the experience of the Christian community in creedal definitions drawn from the terminology of Greek metaphysics. That was the era in which the Holy Spirit became "the Third Person of the Trinity"—a concept that has baffled countless generations of Sunday school classes.

Today theology is breaking out of the prison of Greek thought forms. It also is reacting against the mania for definition which obsessed the church for so many centuries. It is returning to the attitude of the earliest Christians, who were willing to live with mystery, and who knew that experiencing God's presence is infinitely more important than trying to explain it in a neat verbal formula.

Thus it is possible for contemporary theology to speak of the Holy Spirit not in confusing trinitarian language, but simply as God here and now, God at work in the world, God dwelling within the hearts and minds of men.

This is a congenial approach to a pragmatic generation that thinks in terms of results. And it opens up a whole treasury of biblical language for use in answering the religious questions that are actually being asked by young people and adults today.

One of those questions is: How can I know what to believe —about the meaning of life, my relation to the ultimate, about right and wrong?

The Bible's answer is that the Holy Spirit "will lead you into all truth" if given a chance. The Spirit's guidance is freely available to all who seek it. It is usually given not through "voices" or "visions" or other external manifestations, but quietly and naturally from the innermost depths of man's own being.

The Spirit's guidance may be experienced subjectively as "conscience" or as "intuition." In the former aspect, it undergirds man's moral sense. In the latter, it is the wellspring of man's faith that life does have meaning and purpose.

The apostle Paul said the indwelling Spirit is the only real basis human beings have for believing that they are creatures of a benevolent God.

"For the Spirit that God has given you does not make you a slave and cause you to be afraid," he told the Christians at Rome. "Instead, the Spirit makes you God's sons, and by the Spirit's power we cry to God, 'Father, my Father!'"

"Power" is a word frequently used by New Testament authors in conjunction with the Holy Spirit. They recognized that man's biggest religious problem is not knowing what is right, but doing what is right in situations where it would be easier, safer, or more pleasant to do otherwise. Man on his own is a weak, self-centered creature with a vast capacity for rationalization, according to the Bible. It is only "in the power of the Spirit" that man is able to rise above himself and do genuinely good, kind, and courageous things.

One of the great insights of the New Testament which modern theology is recovering is that the Holy Spirit cannot be imprisoned in institutions nor manipulated by rites. Although the church is intended to be the primary locus of the Spirit's activity—"the fellowship of the Holy Spirit" is one of the biblical synonyms for the church—the Spirit also is constantly at work outside the church, in the hearts and minds of men who do not think of themselves as Christians in any sense, and who may not even believe in God.

Sometimes, and many would say that the present is such a time, the reforming, cleansing, healing power of the Spirit may be manifested more dramatically in movements and events that are not specifically religious than within the life of the institutional church itself.

★ Questions to ponder or discuss

Have you ever experienced what you regarded—at the time or upon later reflection—as the guidance or empowerment of the Holy Spirit?

Have you ever been conscious of being strengthened, emboldened or sustained in trouble by what seemed to be a power not of your own?

What is your attitude toward the phenomenon called "glossolalia" or "speaking in tongues"? Does it have any place at all in the contemporary church? Why? Are there dangers in emphasizing the more dramatic gifts of the Spirit?

Is there a worse danger in playing down or ignoring the reality of the Spirit?

Is ecstatic utterance any more of a "miracle"—or indeed as much of a miracle—as the transformation of a human life and character?

14 ☀ Superstition in the Space Age

One of the most curious phenomena of contemporary American life is a tremendous upsurge of public interest in astrology, witchcraft, spiritualism, and other occult arts.

"The present 'occult boom' seems to have tapped a hidden reservoir of the mind," says *Editorial Research Reports*. "Classes in the history of witchcraft, sorcery and the black arts are being taught in many high schools and universities, and they are usually overenrolled. Bookstore shelves are laden with occult books, both sensational and academic. More than 1,200 daily newspapers in the United States publish columns on astrology. . . .

"There is abundant evidence that millions of persons half-believe, are willing to believe, or do indeed believe in mysterious forces that are dismissed by science and most Western religions as superstition."

That such a mass retrogression into ancient idolatries should take place in this supposedly enlightened age is a judgment on America's churches.

It clearly indicates that mainline religious bodies have not been filling a widely and deeply felt need for a transrational dimension to human existence.

David H. C. Read, pastor of Madison Avenue Presbyterian Church in New York, says there is great "yearning for the transcendent," particularly among young people who are in revolt against a secular and materialistic society.

Psychotherapist Ludwig B. Lefebre agrees that vast numbers of people are seeking ways "to get beyond themselves." And most churches, he says, "are not responding adequately" to this hunger for "direct contact with a suprahuman agency."

Since "direct contact with a suprahuman agency" or, in conventional religious language, communion with God—is precisely what churches are supposed to be offering, it is a very serious indictment to say that most of them aren't "responding" to a widespread demand for it.

But churchmen must admit there is considerable truth to the charge. In recent years many theologians, ministers, and laymen have been obsessed with trying to prove to the world that the church is "relevant" to man's everyday secular concerns.

A great effort has been made to de-emphasize the supernatural, "otherworld" aspect of Christian teaching, and to present religion as a here-and-now aid to ethical behavior.

This approach was taken in the confident assumption that it would have far greater appeal to "modern man" than a lot of talk about life after death, prayer, and the felt presence of the Holy Spirit.

But it is beginning to appear that "modern man" is not quite as ready as some theologians thought to reject anything he can't explain on rational grounds. On the contrary, he seems to retain an ineradicable intuition that there is more to this world than is dreamt of in materialistic philosophy and secularized religion.

If churches are too timid to proclaim the reality of this transcendental dimension, they can hardly be surprised to find people turning to psychedelic drugs, mediums, séances, stargazing, sorcery, magical rites, and even such fantastic perversions of spirituality as Satan worship.

Even in the space age, when authentic religion languishes, superstition is waiting in the wings to usurp its place in human life.

★ Questions to ponder or discuss

Why do you think there is so much current interest in spiritualism and the occult?

Have you been attracted to any of these things? Why?

In the church you attend, how much emphasis is placed on direct personal experience of the reality of God as a possibility open to every human being?

15 ☀ *Pointers on Prayer*

A college professor paused to examine the titles on display in the tract rack of his Episcopal church. He visibly recoiled from one little green-and-white pamphlet which he found in a prominent spot. "This," he remarked to a companion, "is carrying the 'how to' craze too far."

The pamphlet was entitled "Instructions in the Life of Prayer."

Many sensitive and intelligent laymen share the professor's distaste for any pamphlet, book, or article which suggests that there are techniques in prayer.

These people love the beautiful and majestic formal prayers which we use in public worship. But they feel that private prayer should be unstudied and unrehearsed, a spontaneous outpouring of the heart to God.

Spiritual directors agree that spontaneous prayer has great value and that it is appropriate for any time, place, or circumstance.

But from the time of Jesus until now, they have also insisted that there are rules to be learned and disciplines to be practiced in prayer. When his disciples said, "Teach us to pray," our Lord did not respond with a lecture on spontaneity.

He gave very explicit and practical advice, including a model prayer.

Over the centuries, hundreds of saints and scholars have contributed to a massive literature on prayer.

Outlined below are seven specific suggestions which have been commended by many Christians through the ages:

Pray each day at the same time. No matter how many spontaneous prayers you may offer during the course of the day, you should also have a fixed, regular time for private prayer. Treat it as the most important appointment in your day and don't let anything intrude upon it or crowd it out. Some people pray best early in the morning, before they are involved in the day's activities. Others prefer to pray before retiring at night. The important thing is to pick a time you can call your own and stick to it every day.

It is helpful to have a regular place as well as a regular time for prayer. It may be any place you find convenient, so long as it affords complete privacy. Jesus recommended a closet. In the modern home or apartment, that might be translated into a bedroom or bathroom. Lock the door if possible. Your ability to concentrate on your prayers is directly related to your assurance that no one will see, overhear, or interrupt you.

The posture you assume in prayer does not matter to God, but it may make a great difference to you. You can stand, sit, kneel, or lie down to pray. Kneeling is a physical act of humility which helps many people to prepare psychologically for prayer. An uncomfortable position may be a distraction, but one that is too comfortable—for example, lying in bed—is likely to lead to drowsiness rather than concentration.

Prepare for prayer with a brief period of devotional reading. This helps you to make the transition from the hectic world of daily routine to the quiet mood of prayer. It enables you to focus your attention on God, an act which is both the precondition and the purpose of prayer.

Pray as long as you need to or want to—and no longer. Jesus warned that long-windedness is not a virtue in prayer, and the model prayer he gave to his disciples has only sixty-seven words. Until you are far advanced in the spiritual life, you may find it difficult to sustain a genuine mood of prayer for longer than five or ten minutes at a stretch. It is better to pray briefly and regularly than to indulge in marathon prayers one day and then skip several days.

Pray whether you "feel like it" or not. It is your will, not your fleeting emotions, which you offer to God in prayer. Even the most saintly go through frequent "dry periods" when they do not feel the least bit prayerful. But they keep on praying.

Do not be ashamed to offer "selfish" prayers, or to seek God's help in "little" things. Jesus included in his model prayer a petition for bread, which is about as mundane a request as you can make. But you shouldn't let personal petitions dominate your prayer. They are likely to do so unless you deliberately practice other kinds.

What other kinds? Spiritual directors have identified four—intercession, confession, thanksgiving, and adoration.

Intercession has been described as "loving your neighbor on your knees." This is the prayer in which you seek God's help for other people. It is important to avoid vague and meaningless generalities ("Please bless the poor and sick") and to pray for the specific needs of specific individuals.

Confession is the prayer in which we acknowledge our sins and accept God's forgiveness of them. Here again, it is better to be specific whenever possible. In confession we humbly and contritely admit that we have become separated from God by our own sinfulness, and we open our lives to the healing, reconciling, restoring, uplifting grace of him who loves us in spite of what we are.

Thanksgiving means counting your blessings. As in the case of intercession and confession, it is always better to be specific

—to thank God sincerely for particular good things in your life. The true spirit of thanksgiving also accepts the adversities of life and sees even in them the merciful if sometimes mysterious hand of a loving Father.

Adoration is the highest form of prayer. It means lifting up your heart to God and saying in whatever words you find most meaningful that you acknowledge him to be worthy of your utmost love and obedience. The Lord's Prayer begins with a simple expression of adoration: "Our Father which art in heaven, hallowed be thy name. Thy kingdom come, thy will be done."

★ Questions to ponder or discuss

How regularly do you pray? Have you ever thought of prayer as a "holy habit" which must be cultivated like any other habit? Would praying at the same time and the same place every day help a person to cultivate the prayer habit?

Analyze the content of your own prayers. What proportions are devoted to petition, intercession, confession, thanksgiving, and adoration? Are there types of prayer in which you rarely or never engage?

16 ※ Praying for Others

Is it right to pray for others? Does it do any good?

Pastors often hear those questions, not from skeptics, but from devout men and women who believe in prayer.

Inquiry usually reveals that they pray regularly for divine guidance and strength to cope with their own problems. But they are hesitant about asking God's help for other people. They feel that such intercessory prayers are unnecessary and perhaps even impertinent.

Their viewpoint was succinctly expressed by a woman who told her minister: "I would never presume to call God's attention to somebody else's troubles. I figure he knows their needs better than I do, and that he loves them more than I possibly can."

It is a persuasive argument, as far as it goes. But its conclusion is repudiated by 2,000 years of Christian tradition.

From the time of the New Testament apostles until now, the Christian church has ascribed great value to intercessory prayer.

It has taught—and many individuals have confirmed in their own experience—that praying for others is always helpful to the one who does the praying.

"We pray for the people we love," explains one Christian writer. "But it works the other way, too. We come to love the people we pray for. When you find yourself inclined to hate someone, try praying for him. You'll find that it changes your whole attitude toward him. That's what Jesus meant when he commanded his disciples to pray for their enemies."

Other Christian teachers refer to intercessory prayer as "the school of charity." They say that every sincere petition for the welfare of another human being carries with it the implied offer to serve as God's instrument in the matter. Thus people who make a habit of praying for others inevitably find themselves becoming more sensitive to the needs of everyone around them, and more generous in responding.

If Christians were content to rest the case at this point, there might be little controversy over the value of intercessory prayer. The psychological impact of prayer on the person praying is widely acknowledged today even by those who do not believe that prayers are "answered" in any other way.

But throughout its history, the church has made another claim for intercessory prayers. It has said that they sometimes have very remarkable effects in the lives of the persons prayed for.

This claim is offensive to some people, not because they disbelieve in God, but because they cannot accept the idea that he intervenes unpredictably in the orderly working of his creation. To these people, it seems more reverent to think of God as the Author of immutable natural laws than to ascribe to him occasional "miracles" which seem to involve the setting aside of those laws.

C. S. Lewis acknowledged that there may be a "theoretical problem" in believing that "God ever really modifies his action in response to the suggestions of men."

"Infinite wisdom does not need telling what is best, and infinite goodness needs no urging to do it," said Lewis. "But neither does God need any of those other things that are done by finite agents, whether living or inanimate. He could, if he chose, repair our bodies miraculously without food; or give us food without the aid of farmers, bakers and butchers; or knowledge without the aid of learned men; or convert the heathen without missionaries. Instead, he allows soils and weather and animals and the muscles, minds and wills of men to cooperate in the execution of his will."

He concuded that "it is not really stranger that my prayers should affect the course of events than that my other actions should do so."

George MacDonald, the great nineteenth-century Scottish preacher, had a more eloquent answer to the belief that the universe is inexorable in its flow of cause and effect:

"Does God care for suns and planets and satellites, for divine mathematics and ordered harmonies, more than for his children? If his machine interfered with his answering the prayer of a single child, he would sweep it from him—not to bring back chaos, but to make room for his child."

Whether it is theoretically "strange" or perfectly natural that God should answer prayers, millions of people through the ages have been absolutely convinced by their own experience that he does in fact do so.

"We do not know in every instance precisely how God acts in response to our prayers," says Episcopal theologian John B. Coburn. "Indeed, we do not know why it is that apparently some prayers are answered immediately and just as we hoped they would be, while others seemingly are not answered for years, and then only in ways we did not expect.

"But, within the mystery that surrounds intercessory prayer, we can affirm one great certainty. When we pray, things happen that would not otherwise happen."

The skeptic may dismiss the apparent results of intercessory prayer as pure coincidence, and it is difficult to conceive of any kind of external evidence that would disprove this contention in any particular case.

But the fact remains, as the late Archbishop William Temple once observed, that "when you stop praying, coincidences stop happening."

★ Questions to ponder or discuss

What is your attitude toward intercessory prayer? Do you practice it? Why?

What is your explanation for the fact that God seems to grant some prayers and say no to others? Is personal righteousness any assurance that God will grant your requests? If so, how do you account for the fact that Jesus himself got no for an answer when he prayed in Gethsemane to be delivered from the agony of the cross?

Do you believe that God can, if he chooses, intervene in the ordinary workings of nature to bring about what would be regarded at the human level as a "miracle"? Why?

17 🌟 Prepackaged Prayers

The best prayers are those that rise spontaneously from the human heart at moments of great need, penitence, or gratitude.

They require few words: "Help me . . . forgive me . . . thank you."

To acknowledge the supremacy of spontaneous prayers, however, is not to say that men can get along without more formal prayers which have been thought out and written down in advance.

Prepackaged prayer has two great merits. It is a way of reaching out toward God in hours of spiritual drought. And it can serve to remind us of dimensions of need, forms of guilt, or occasions for thankfulness that may have escaped our attention.

The greatest and most widely used formal prayer is the one that Jesus taught his disciples. Here is a new ecumenical translation that has been prepared by Protestant and Catholic scholars:

> *Our Father in heaven, holy be your name,*
> *Your kingdom come, your will be done,*

On earth as in heaven.
Give us today our daily bread.
Forgive us our sins as we forgive those
who sin against us.
Do not bring us to the test,
But deliver us from evil.
For the kingdom, the power and the glory
are yours, now and for ever.

The gentle and Christlike Francis of Assisi is the author of two prayers which men have found perennially pertinent to their needs.

One is very brief:

O God, help me to want to love you.

The other, somewhat longer, is St. Francis' famous Peace Prayer:

Lord, make me an instrument of thy peace.
Where there is hatred, let me sow love;
Where there is injury, pardon;
Where there is doubt, faith;
Where there is despair, hope;
Where there is darkness, light;
And where there is sickness, joy.
O Divine Master, grant that I may not so
much seek to be consoled as to console;
To be understood as to understand;
To be loved as to love;
For it is in giving that we receive; it
is in pardoning that we are pardoned;
and it is in dying that we are born to
eternal life. Amen.

The great sculptor Michelangelo was a devout man driven by tumultuous passions. In his diary was found this prayer:

Lord, on you I call for help against my blind and senseless torment, since you alone can renew inwardly and outwardly my mind, my will, and my strength, which are weak.

The Book of Common Prayer contains some of the most apt and eloquent prayers ever written. They cover every conceivable occasion in human life from birth to death. Some of them are surprisingly relevant to modern concerns despite their antiquity. Here is a prayer for social justice:

Almighty God, who hast created man in thine own image; Grant us grace fearlessly to contend against evil, and to make no peace with oppression; and, that we may reverently use our freedom, help us to employ it in the maintenance of justice among men and nations, to the glory of thy holy Name; through Jesus Christ our Lord, Amen.

One of the world's best-loved devotional books is *A Diary of Private Prayer* by Scottish theologian John Baillie. Here is an excerpt from Baillie's "Prayer of Repentance":

My failure to be true even to my own accepted standards:
My self-deception in the face of temptation:
My choosing of the worse when I know the better:
O Lord, forgive.
My failure to apply to myself the standards of conduct I demand of others;
My blindness to the suffering of others and my slowness to be taught by my own:

*My complacence towards wrongs that do not touch
my own case and my over-sensitiveness to those that do:
My slowness to see the good in my fellows and
to see the evil in myself:
My hardness of heart towards my neighbor's
faults and my readiness to make allowance for my own:
My unwillingness to believe that thou hast
called me to a small work and my brother to a great one:
O Lord, forgive.*

★ Questions to ponder or discuss

What is your own feeling about the use of prayers composed by others?

Have you ever tried to use such prayers in your private devotions, taking care to identify yourself with the thoughts and petitions they express, so that they become in a real sense your own prayers?

Browse through the book of Psalms. How many passages can you find that might be used as prayers in your own private devotions? Do you find some of them remarkably relevant to current human problems?

18 ❄ *Is the Church Obsolete?*

It's easy to criticize the church.

At any time and in any place, men can justly accuse the church of failing to live up to its own teachings. The charge is always correct, to some degree, because the church proclaims ideals of unselfishness, love, and service which no group of human beings can perfectly achieve.

As an antidote to complacency and a spur to greater effort, criticism of the church can be a healthy thing. When it's overdone, it becomes merely destructive.

It's one thing to say the church has shortcomings, which it certainly has. It's quite a different thing to suggest—as many now are doing—that the church is obsolete, useless, and expendable.

It has become fashionable, among young people and among some of the clergy, to speak of the church as an institution whose disappearance would do no great harm and might even be beneficial to the furtherance of the ideals and way of life associated with Jesus Christ.

History says otherwise. From the time of Jesus until now, Christian living has been an adventure in which men and women have found it necessary to have company. It is difficult enough to be a real Christian when you have people around you who share your commitment and conviction, people on whom you can rely for support and encouragement, and who rely in turn on you. Without much mutual reinforcement, fidelity to the way of Christ is virtually impossible.

Jesus recognized this. The first act of his ministry was to call together a little band of disciples to be his constant companions. It is quite clear from the Gospels that Jesus didn't look upon his disciples merely as students to learn and relay his teaching. They were his friends. He needed them, even as they needed him.

And that, of course, is what the church still is supposed to be—not just an institution with worthy objectives, but a fellowship, a brotherhood, an ongoing community which transcends all barriers of time and space.

The mission of this community is twofold, and is plainly spelled out in the Bible. It is to nurture, sustain, and instruct those already included in its membership. And it is to reach out with love and humility to render whatever service it can to the rest of mankind.

How well the church performs its mission at any particular place and time depends not on how large and powerful and rich it is, but rather on the degree to which its members are genuinely committed to the role of a servant community.

There always have been, and always will be, some men and women conspicuously attached to the Christian community and active in its internal affairs who have never really understood what Jesus was talking about. But their presence in the mix does not invalidate the original idea. They merely make it more difficult for the church to be the church.

The church has endured for 2,000 years, and I believe will always endure, because it also has managed to maintain, in every generation, a cadre of genuinely committed Christians—men and women so much in love with God, so sincerely concerned for their brother's welfare, that they are prepared to be obedient, as Jesus was, unto death.

It is amazing how much can be accomplished by even a small group of people who have fully accepted Jesus' challenge to "take up your cross and follow me." Those who wring their hands over statistics indicating the church is losing members and influence should bear this in mind.

It is not through great size, nor weight of numbers, nor wealth, but solely through commitment, that the church is able to stand forth among men in the high and holy role of the Body of Christ.

The critics are right when they say there is much about the contemporary church that is unlovely and unchristlike. What they do not always seem to understand is that there ultimately is only one way in which the church can be reformed and strengthened—by individuals daring to become real Christians.

★ Questions to ponder or discuss

In your opinion, what would happen to Christianity if the church should "wither away" as some have recently prophesied?

Is the Old Testament story of Gideon's Army (which you'll find in the sixth, seventh, and eighth chapters of the book of Judges) relevant to the contemporary situation of the Christian church?

What are *you* doing to strengthen the church?

19 ☀ *Believing and Doing*

Many people equate religion with acceptance of certain doctrines.

But this is not the biblical view. In the great source book of Judaism and Christianity, a religious person is distinguished not by his stated beliefs but by his actions, his attitudes, his relationships—in short, by his style of life.

It is of course true that everyone's style of life ultimately reflects his deepest convictions. But what a person says is not always a reliable guide to what he believes strongly enough to live by. Some who profess ardent religious faith are unwilling to take any costly or dangerous action in obedience to that faith. And many who call themselves unbelievers display in actual practice a profound commitment to the values which biblical religion upholds.

Anyone who thinks that religion is merely a matter of "believing in God" will find little comfort in the Scriptures.

"So you believe that there is one God?" asks the author of the New Testament Epistle of James. "Good for you! The demons also believe that—and shudder."

Hundreds of years earlier, the great Jewish prophets had

warned that God is concerned with the way men act rather than their diligence in paying ritual tributes to him.

"Thus says the Lord," cried the prophet Amos:

> *I hate, I despise your feasts,*
> *and I take no delight in your solemn assemblies. . . .*
> *Take away from me the noise of your songs;*
> *to the melody of your harps I will not listen.*
> *But let justice roll down like waters,*
> *and righteousness like an ever-flowing stream.*

The prophet Micah was equally scornful of a "religion" which expresses itself only in giving lip service to orthodox beliefs and attending punctiliously to ceremonies which are thought to honor God.

"With what shall I come before the Lord, and bow myself before God on high?" Micah asked.

> *Shall I come before him with burnt offerings? . . .*
> *Will the Lord be pleased with thousands of rams,*
> *with ten thousand rivers of oil? . . .*
> *He has showed you, O man, what is good;*
> *And what does the Lord require of you,*
> *but to do justice, and to love kindness,*
> *and to walk humbly with your God?*

Perhaps the most persistent of all Christian heresies is the idea that a person is assured of salvation if he publicly professes belief that Jesus is the Son of God.

Jesus gave no encouragement to that kind of purely verbal piety.

"Not every person who calls me 'Lord, Lord' will enter into the Kingdom of heaven, but only those who do what my Father in heaven wants them to do," he said in the Sermon on the Mount.

On another occasion, when some of his disciples were proclaiming their devotion to him, he told them they could easily prove it by their deeds.

"If you really love me," he said, "you will obey my commandments."

No one attached greater importance to faith than the apostle Paul. But in his letter to Christians at Rome, he said that true worship consists of offering yourself as a "living sacrifice to God."

"Love one another warmly as brothers in Christ, and be eager to show respect for one another," he said. "Work hard, and do not be lazy. Serve the Lord with a heart full of devotion, . . . share your belongings with your needy brothers, and open your homes to strangers. . . .

"Do not be proud but accept humble duties. Do not think of yourselves as wise.

"If someone does evil to you, do not pay him back with evil. Try to do what all men consider to be good. Do everything possible, on your part, to live at peace with all men."

Reread that passage and note the active verbs: love . . . work . . . serve . . . share . . . accept . . . try . . . do.

The biblical emphasis on doing reaches a climax in the Epistle of James.

"Do not fool yourselves by just listening to God's word," it admonishes. "Instead, put it into practice. . . .

"What good is it for a man to say, 'I have faith,' if his actions do not prove it?. . . Show me how you can have faith without actions; I will show you my faith by my actions."

★ Questions to ponder or discuss

William Temple, the late Archbishop of Canterbury, once said: "I expect to meet in heaven many who now call themselves atheists." Do you agree with the implication of this remark?

Has the religious training you've received—in Sunday school or wherever—given you the impression that God is more concerned with whether men believe in his existence than with how they treat each other?

Has the church lost ground with young people of our time by trying to show the world "faith without works"?

20 ☀ It Takes Two Sides to Make a Coin

Controversy over social action is gravely disrupting many churches.

Not since fundamentalists and modernists battled in the 1920s over infallibility of the Bible has there been such a deep, emotional division in American church life.

Cutting across denominational lines, it affects virtually every major religious body. And, like politics, it makes strange bedfellows. A Roman Catholic and a Southern Baptist committed to social action may find themselves in greater rapport than either feels with members of his own denomination who oppose church involvement in public affairs.

As often happens in a highly charged dispute, each side tends to caricature the position of the other. A rabid activist may imply that people on the other side are indifferent to human suffering. An agitated conservative may suggest that the social action movement is so preoccupied with man's problems that it ignores God. Such extreme statements add to the confusion of the man in the pew who's trying to figure out what the row is all about.

Actually, neither side is as single-minded as the opposition paints it.

The Rev. Billy Graham is one of the most articulate exponents of the view that the church is "in danger of moving off the main track and getting lost on a siding" if it becomes too deeply involved in "trying to solve every ill of society."

But even as he insists that "the changing of men's hearts is the primary mission of the church," Dr. Graham adds that there also is "a sense in which the church is to advise, warn and challenge society" by proclaiming God's judgments on its evils and "by preaching the whole counsel of God, which involves man's environment and physical being as well as his soul."

No one has better credentials as a social action advocate than the Rt. Rev. Paul Moore, Jr., Episcopalian, Bishop of New York. But Bishop Moore says:

"I resist with all my being the church becoming just a social action or service institution.

"Without the life of worship at its heart, social work and action can soon lose vitality, or become bitter and violent. On the other hand, the church without social involvement soon becomes a place of false spirituality divorced from the flesh which God put on in Jesus Christ."

That Paul Moore and Billy Graham are equally dedicated Christians, this writer can testify from long personal acquaintance with both men. Each of them is trying his level best to lead the church in the direction he believes Jesus Christ would have it move. They simply happen to disagree about what that direction is.

Dr. Graham wants to see poverty, war, and discrimination eliminated as much as Bishop Moore does. But he is convinced that the only way to change human society is to change individual men by converting them to Jesus Christ.

Bishop Moore believes in the lordship and saving power of Christ as earnestly as Dr. Graham does. But he is convinced that human needs, for which Christ showed unfailing compassion, can be effectively relieved in the modern world only by men of good will working together in social and political action.

There are millions of church members who share each of these viewpoints.

It would be a great tragedy if this honest difference of opinion should degenerate into a nasty squabble which creates the impression that the church faces an "either-or" choice between evangelism and social action. The plain truth is that Jesus was concerned with both the spiritual and the material welfare of human beings, and his church cannot afford to neglect *either* of these concerns.

★ Questions to ponder or discuss

Do you feel that the church today is more deeply involved in social and political concerns than it should be? Why? Or would you rather see it become even more active in the fight for a better society? Why?

Samuel Johnson, the great English lexicographer, once found himself in the company of a man given to dogmatic assertions. In a desperate effort to get his companion to open his mind, Dr. Johnson cried: "I beseech you, sir, by the mercies of Christ, consider the possibility that you may be mistaken!" Is this sound advice for all parties to the controversy over social action? Do you follow it?

21 ⚜ Putting Up with Each Other

In listing the hallmarks of Christian character, St. Paul gave prominent mention to the virtue of forbearance.

It is a virtue much needed but little practiced in America today.

Forbearance is patience under provocation.

It is controlling your impulse to anger when somebody says or does something you don't like.

It is being slow to condemn the motives of others, even when their conduct seems outrageous.

Instead of "forbearing one another and forgiving one another," as Paul enjoined, many of us in contemporary America have fallen into a harshly judgmental temper.

We are continually weighing one another and finding one another wanting.

Young people are judgmental toward their elders, whom they call square, hypocritical, and materialistic.

Elders are judgmental toward young people, whom they call irresponsible, self-righteous, and impractical.

White people accuse black people of being shiftless, prone to crime, full of demands but unwilling to work up the hard way.

Black people accuse white people of being greedy, blind to their own sins, full of exhortations but unwilling to give minorities a fair chance.

Even within the church there is an acrid atmosphere of mutual condemnation.

Liberals condemn conservatives for resisting reforms needed to make religion relevant to modern man.

Conservatives condemn liberals for jettisoning essential parts of the gospel in their frantic quest for the approval of a skeptical society.

Laymen berate clergymen for neglecting the cure of souls in their preoccupation with social action.

Clergymen upbraid laymen for neglecting the welfare of their fellowman in their preoccupation with individual piety.

You could go on expanding the list indefinitely. Intramural conflict is perhaps the most conspicuous feature of our national life in the last third of the twentieth century.

No individual can change all of this, but each of us can begin to minimize our personal contribution to it.

Those who profess the Name of Christ should find sufficient inducement in his teaching.

"Do not judge others, and God will not judge you," Jesus said. "Do not condemn others, and God will not condemn you. Forgive others, and God will forgive you. The measure you use for others is the measure God will use for you."

★ Questions to ponder or discuss

Are you entirely comfortable with the thought that God will be precisely as forgiving toward you as you are toward people who wrong you?

Have you encountered people who feel it is their Christian duty to condemn wrongdoers?

If we all followed Jesus' counsel never to condemn another

87

person, what difference would it make in family life? In relationships among friends and neighbors? In public life and politics?

Read Luke 6:41-42. Is this saying of Jesus also relevant here?

22 ☀ *Strength in Weakness*

One of the most astounding paradoxes of Christian teaching is the assertion that in weakness there is strength.

Conventional wisdom takes exactly the opposite view. To be weak, it says, is to be helpless, ineffective, frustrated, and despised. It is to invite trampling by the strong.

The world in which the apostle Paul lived—the world of the first-century Roman Empire—was even more ruthless, more oriented toward power, than our own.

Yet it was Paul who said: "When I am weak, then I am strong."

No casual observer would have described Paul as weak. He was one of the most dynamic human beings who ever lived, a man of enormous vitality, courage, and endurance. He had a brilliant mind. Moreover, he knew himself to be extraordinarily gifted.

And that is why he needed the experience of weakness in order to become truly strong.

Paul explained it in one of his letters to the church at Corinth with his usual blunt candor.

"To keep me from being puffed up with pride . . . I was given a painful physical ailment," he said.

Interpreters have been speculating for twenty centuries about the precise nature of Paul's physical handicap. One popular theory is that he suffered from epilepsy. Another is that he was subject to migraine headaches. One imaginative scholar has suggested that perhaps he was just terribly ugly.

Paul supplied no clues. He referred to his physical infirmity only as "Satan's messenger to beat me and keep me from being proud."

Paul had seen many sick people get well when he laid his hands upon them and prayed for their recovery in the name of the Lord Jesus Christ. But when he sought healing for himself, he got no for an answer.

"Three times I prayed to the Lord about this, and asked him to take my infirmity away," he told the Corinthians.

But the Lord's answer was: "My grace is all you need; for my power is strongest when you are weak."

Paul finally was able to accept the answer. He came to realize that he needed his handicap to keep him from thinking that he could make it by himself, and to remind him of his dependence on God as the ultimate source of his spiritual strength.

He learned at last, he told the Corinthians, to rejoice in his infirmity because it enabled him to "feel the protection of Christ's power over me."

Paul knew better than most people that this "protection" did not mean that he would be spared from pain, suffering, hardship, poverty, loneliness, and persecution. The idea that God "takes care" of those who believe in him by giving them a soft ride in this world was totally foreign to the teaching and example of Christ—and to the daily experience of the early church.

The protective power of which Paul spoke was the inner strength—the peace, the joy, the capacity for love and kindness—which God confers upon those who know they are powerless, without his help, to do any good thing.

Many ordinary folk since the time of Paul have made the same discovery—that real strength begins on the far side of acknowledged helplessness. Indeed, this is one of the cardinal principles of Alcoholics Anonymous, which has had remarkable success in reclaiming some very wonderful people from life's scrap heap.

★ Questions to ponder or discuss

May an earnest striving for moral perfection become a *barrier* rather than a pathway to increased knowledge of God?

Read Luke 18:9-14. Does this parable of Jesus shed any light on the dangers inherent in a self-conscious posture of moral rectitude?

Have you ever been in such great trouble, or in such despair over your own failures and imperfections, that you knew there was absolutely nothing you could do about the situation except to place it in God's hands? Would you be willing to be brought to such a low point in order to experience the presence and power of God in a most vivid and direct way?

What did the author of the ninety-fourth psalm mean by saying, "Blessed is the man whom thou dost chasten, O Lord"?

23 ❊ Is Anybody Out There?

Will space-venturing man find intelligent life on other planets?

If he does, what impact will the discovery have on his religious beliefs?

These questions have come in for much discussion since men began to walk on the moon and to plan visits to more distant bodies.

But the advent of manned space flight does *not* presage an early answer to the question whether life exists in other parts of the universe besides earth.

Leading astronomers like Harlow Shapley of Harvard and F. B. Hoyle of Cambridge say that there are probably millions of planets in the universe where conditions are suitable for the existence of living creatures.

But they also say that the earth appears to be the only planet in our solar system which has the kind of atmosphere, moisture, and orbit necessary to sustain life.

This means that man will have to travel, not merely to Mars, but to another solar system before there is any likelihood of his coming face to face with other living beings.

A trip to Mars is not inconceivable, since that planet at times comes within thirty-five million miles of earth. But distances of incredibly greater magnitude are involved in getting to another solar system. The nearest solar system is about twenty-seven trillion miles away. At a speed of twenty-five thousand miles an hour, a manned space vehicle would need more than one hundred thousand years to get there.

So it may be a very long time, if ever, before man knows for sure whether there is "life out yonder."

Assuming that there is—and many theologians are quite as willing as astronomers to make this assumption—what implication does this have for religious belief?

Skeptics have said that the discovery of life on other planets would tend to discredit the belief, basic to all religious faith, that God is concerned with the hopes and fears and moral strivings of the human creatures who inhabit this particular speck of matter in his vast universe.

If life exists widely throughout the universe, the skeptics ask, is it not the height of arrogance to claim—as Christians do claim—that God cares so much about man that he once became incarnate in a human personality in order to lead man back to the way, the truth, and the life?

In reply to such challenges, Christian scholars make these points:

Those who believe that an omnipotent God is capable of taking a personal, fatherly interest in each of the nearly three billion human creatures now living on earth should have no difficulty in stretching their earthbound imaginations to include the possibility that he is equally concerned with any multiple of that number on other planets.

If there are rational beings elsewhere in the universe who are in a "fallen" spiritual state like man, there is nothing in Christian theology which denies the possibility that God may have acted to redeem them, as he acted to redeem man in the person of Jesus Christ. Centuries ago, Thomas Aquinas discussed the possibility of other incarnations of God, for the benefit of other creatures than man.

Indeed, there is traceable in Christian literature a recurrent intuition that the redemptive work of Christ was *not* confined to earth. This belief existed long before the advent of space travel.

★ Questions to ponder or discuss

How would you personally react to an official announcement that radiotelescopes had picked up emissions from distant space which had every appearance of being messages transmitted by intelligent beings? Would you feel that this constituted a threat to your religious faith? Why?

J. B. Phillips, the great English Bible translator, once wrote a book entitled *Your God Is Too Small*. Does this strike you as an accurate statement about most of us? Do we have a tendency, even in this space age, to go on thinking about God as a finite being who lives somewhere "up there" above our own planet? Why does this inadequate image of God persist? Is it because we don't stop very often to *think* about God, or to meditate on his majesty as Author and Sustainer of the whole universe?

24 ☀ Is Death the End of the Line?

"What happens when I die?"

Man is the only creature who asks that question. But he asks it very insistently. It has bothered him since the dawn of human history. It is perhaps the most basic question he asks of any religion or philosophy which professes to help him comprehend the meaning of his existence.

There are four possible answers, and each of them has many adherents.

One theory is that death is the end of the line for human beings, as for other organisms. Life simply ceases to exist and the indefinable essence which constitutes a human personality is swallowed up by nothingness. This is what millions of secularists believe. It is not a modern idea. It is one of the oldest, if not the oldest, of man's guesses about death.

Also of great antiquity is the belief that man has a soul which is imperishable by its very nature. At death, this immortal part of every human being is liberated from the physical body which undergoes corruption. This is what Plato, Socrates, and other Greek philosophers believed. Their view is held today by many who mistakenly regard it as a Christian concept.

A third hypothesis is that a soul may inhabit a succession of physical bodies—animal or human. When one body dies, the soul is "reincarnated" or reborn in another body. This is the teaching of the great Oriental religions, Hinduism and Buddhism. It should be noted that both of them look upon reincarnation as a fate to be avoided if possible. The best thing that can happen to a soul, they believe, is to be released from the cycle of rebirth, to cease to exist as a separate entity and be absorbed into the "oversoul" of Infinite Being "like a drop of water disappearing into the sea."

Finally, there is the Christian viewpoint. It is summarized in the Apostles' Creed by the words: "I believe in . . . the resurrection of the body: and the life everlasting." In theory, it is the most widely professed of the four attitudes; in fact, it is the most widely misunderstood.

Contrary to widespread impression, Christianity does not go along with the Greek philosophers in drawing a sharp distinction between soul and body. It looks upon the human personality as an integrated whole. That is what the Apostles' Creed means by "resurrection of the body." Christians have never thought that existing physical bodies would be restored after death. Paul scouted that idea twenty centuries ago with the scornful remark that flesh and blood cannot inherit the kingdom of God. The "body" to which the Creed refers is a spiritual rather than a physical one. The essential point of the Christian doctrine is that human beings will maintain their separate identities—including self-awareness and the ability to communicate in some fashion with others.

In short, Christianity asserts that what is essential in a person's humanity—the core of his being as a unique individual—will not perish at death but will enter into a new dimension of life beyond the categories of time and space.

Christianity has never claimed that its viewpoint is the most plausible of the four. Christian belief in life after death is based not on logic, but on an event. Twenty centuries ago, on the first Good Friday, the disciples of Jesus Christ saw him crucified, dead, and buried. Three days later, on the first Easter, they saw him alive again.

Their eyewitness testimony has been rejected by many people, in every generation from then until now. These skeptics refuse to consider the historical evidence for the resurrection because they have made up their minds in advance that it couldn't have happened.

Others in every generation have found the testimony convincing. And their initial act of faith in the truthfulness of the disciples' story has been corroborated, they feel, by their own experience of the Christ who can still be encountered at work in the world, not as a memory, but as a living presence.

★ Questions to ponder or discuss

What is your personal theory about what happens after death?

On what logic, intuition, or authority is your belief based? Have you really thought the matter through or is it something you tend to put quickly out of your mind?

Canon C. Leslie Glenn of Washington Cathedral once concluded an Easter sermon with these words: "If you find it difficult to believe the Christian promise of new life after death, allow your mind to dwell occasionally on the possibility that you may be very pleasantly surprised." Can anyone deny that is at least a *possibility*? Even as a mere possibility, does it not irradiate human life with more hope and meaning than it could otherwise have?

25 ☀ Heaven and Hell

Heaven and hell are usually conceived as alternate possibilities, so you might expect that a person who believes in one also would affirm the existence of the other.

But it doesn't always work out that way.

A survey conducted by George Gallup revealed that 68 percent of the American people believe in heaven, but only 54 percent are persuaded of the reality of hell.

The difference between the two figures may be taken as a gauge of the great repugnance which the concept of eternal punishment excites in many otherwise orthodox Christians.

They cannot believe that the loving, merciful, forgiving God revealed by Jesus Christ would consign any poor wretch to a place of perpetual torment.

But Christians who'd like to abandon the idea of hell are confronted with two serious difficulties.

First, there is the teaching of Christ. No responsible biblical scholarship can excise from the Gospels all the passages in which Jesus speaks of the perdition awaiting those who are unloving toward their fellowman and willfully disobedient toward God.

Second, there is the doctrine of free will, which is at the

heart of all biblical religion. It holds that God has given human beings freedom of choice. If this freedom is to be real, it obviously must include the possibility that a particular soul may utterly and finally reject the love of God.

Some theologians have sought a way out of the dilemma by suggesting that sinners may get a second chance for repentance after death. When all the handicaps, limitations, and illusions of earthly life are stripped away, they say, even the most perverse soul will recognize and respond to God's love.

(This, incidentally, is not a modern idea. Several passages in the New Testament indicate that it was held by the apostle Paul.)

Other theologians insist that Christians cannot rule out the possibility, however hypothetical, that some individual may refuse reconciliation with God, no matter how many chances he is given.

But they point out that such a person would not be "sent to hell" by God, but would simply exercise his right as a free spirit to choose eternal separation from God.

Many who hold this view reject the popular image of hell as a place of perpetual torment. The Very Rev. Henry N. Hancock, Dean of St. Mark's Episcopal Cathedral in Minneapolis, has analyzed all the Gospel passages in which Jesus speaks of hell in terms of fire and everlasting punishment. In trying to understand the figures of speech used by Jesus, Dean Hancock says, "It may help if we remember that fire is used primarily for two purposes—either to refine and purify as with metals, or else to destroy as with discarded refuse.

"Moreover, the word translated 'hell' in our English Bible is a reference to the gorge or valley of Gehenna on the west side of Jerusalem where the refuse of the city was (and still is) burned in fires which, quite literally, never go out.

"The thought behind this metaphor, therefore, is not torture but either purification or destruction; and unless we assume,

99

quite unwarrantedly, that what is cast into the fire is indestructible, then it will not burn forever, but will be destroyed."

As for New Testament references to "everlasting punishment," Dean Hancock says: "Obviously utter destruction or annihilation *is* an everlasting punishment in the sense of loss of being; but it is not an unending torment, which is quite another thing."

"A genuinely ethical faith must insist that the way of transgressors, in a rationally ordered universe, is of necessity hard," he concludes. "A creed constructed to comfort the careless cannot be a morally sound creed. We need to contemplate the possibility of hell, not for others but for ourselves, as a warning of the spiritual risks we run whenever we are deliberately disloyal to what we know to be the best."

★ Questions to ponder or discuss

Have you had difficulty trying to reconcile the traditional Christian teaching about a Last Judgment with the concept of God as an infinitely merciful and loving Father?

What solution, if any, have you found?

The concept of purgatory as a state after death in which souls are purified through suffering in preparation for eternal life in heaven is usually rejected by Protestants as a Roman Catholic idea. In the light of Dean Hancock's comments about fire as a purifier, should we perhaps re-examine this attitude? Does *temporary* punishment for corrective purposes sound more like the sort of thing a loving Father might inflict than eternal unending torment?

26 ✵ *The Perils of Being Rich*

Jesus once observed that it is very hard for a rich man to enter the kingdom of heaven.

It is clear from the context that the remark was not meant as a condemnation of rich men. It was a warning that affluence has enormous power to distract men from love of God and love of neighbor.

Anyone who doubts the truth of that statement should take a good hard look at contemporary America.

In our time incomes have soared to the highest level in history. Even a middle-income American family today enjoys luxuries beyond the dreams of the Caesars.

But as living standards have gone up, church attendance has gone down. Pastors detect, especially among young people, a growing disinterest in religious questions—a "who needs God?" attitude.

Many factors doubtless are involved in this turning away. But easy-come, easy-go money certainly is one of them.

One of the pitfalls of affluence is the temptation to regard your prosperity as the well-deserved fruit of your own labor and ingenuity.

This attitude is wanting in gratitude and humility. It fails to acknowledge the large part played in any man's success by happy accidents, by the help of others, and above all, by God-given talents and opportunities.

A variation—equally prideful—is the view that wealth is a gift from God in reward for superior virtue.

Actually, Christian teaching offers no encouragement for the notion that goodness leads to prosperity. A blameless life of love and service led Jesus through trials and troubles to an agonizing death on the cross. And Jesus plainly warned his disciples, at his last supper with them, that if they were really true to his way, "the world will make you suffer."

Perhaps the greatest spiritual danger of prosperity is that it tends to harden human hearts against the needs of others.

How many times have you heard a person of comfortable means express the view that poor people could make it, too, if they'd only get off their lazy bottoms and go to work?

To depict poverty as just punishment for shiftlessness is a blanket judgment sharply contradicted by all that social scientists have discovered in recent years about the handicaps which bear upon the poor from the very hour of birth.

It also is directly contrary to the teaching of Jesus. He warned men repeatedly against being self-righteous, judgmental, and insensitive to the needs of others.

In only one of his many parables did Jesus speak of an individual going to hell. And that individual was a rich man who had no sympathy for a beggar who starved to death at his gate.

★ Questions to ponder or discuss

Do you think of yourself as being rich? Are you more conscious of the relatively few who have more than you do than you are of the many millions around the world who have far less?

Does everyone get more or less what he deserves out of life?

Or do some of us get a lot better break than others, through no particular merit of our own?

Do you know what real poverty is like? From hearsay or personal experience?

Have you heard (or told) stories about people on welfare which imply that most of them are lazy freeloaders? Have you made a serious effort to ascertain the actual facts?

Read Luke 16:19-31. Does this parable of Jesus make you a trifle uneasy in conscience? Should it?

27 ✺ *It Helps Just to Listen*

There are many ways in which one human being can minister to the needs of another.

Feeding the hungry, housing the homeless, healing the sick are traditional "ministries of mercy" well known to everyone.

But you seldom hear anyone mention the ministry of listening.

Because listening seems to be purely passive, we don't realize it can be an act of kindness.

Yet there are many occasions when it's the most helpful thing you can do for a person in trouble.

When you really listen to someone, more than your ears are involved. Your heart has to be engaged, too. To listen, in a true sense, is to open yourself up to another person, and take his pains or troubles or bewilderments into yourself.

Many genuinely compassionate people make poor listeners. They are so anxious to correct the problem that's causing pain they begin to break in with advice and solutions before they've heard the whole story.

Veteran listeners say this is bad form. It's their experience that when a person confides in you, he usually doesn't want advice; he wants somebody to understand and care about his troubles.

Sometimes—as in the case of a person who is grieving over the death of a loved one—there's really nothing you can do to "solve" the problem. Any effort to distract a friend from his grief will only make him feel more lonely because it will convince him that you really don't comprehend how he feels.

In such situations, listening requires a willingness to suffer silently with the grieving friend, accepting not only the reality but also the insolubility of his problem.

Another essential aspect of the art of listening, according to expert practitioners, is the ability to suspend moral judgments.

Some morally upright people find this quite difficult. They feel that if they keep quiet when another person confesses a misdeed or unworthy motive, their silence may be construed as tacit approval.

But no less a moral authority than Jesus of Nazareth refuted the notion that we are required to condemn any course of action which we cannot in good conscience condone. The basic rule laid down by Jesus was: "Do not judge others."

When you listen to a person's troubles in silent sympathy, restraining the impulse to offer good advice or moral counsel, you show him that you care for him, and that you accept him for what he is.

To care and to accept are to love, so listening is an act of love. Indeed, it may be a more intimate act of love—in the sense of establishing true human contact at a deep level— than a purely physical sexual encounter.

In contemporary urban society, where relationships between people seem to be growing ever more impersonal and dehumanized, there is great need for the ministry of listening.

The beauty of it is that this is one form of service that no one is too old or sick or poor or weak to undertake. The feeblest and frailest person can listen—and in doing so, can give to others the benison of knowing that somebody cares.

105

★ Questions to ponder or discuss

What makes a "good listener?"

Have you ever thought of listening as an art that has to be learned and deliberately practiced?

When you tell someone about your troubles, do you want him to advise you how to handle them? To minimize your problems and tell you to "cheer up"? Or are you mainly seeking a little sympathetic understanding of the fact that you have real troubles?

Do you treat others as you wish to be treated in this regard?

28 ☀ Man's Deepest Question: Does Life Have a Meaning?

Ever since he became fully human, about 100,000 years ago, man has asked the deep existential questions: Who am I? Why am I here? What is the meaning of life?

Through the ages, he has come up with many different answers. But not until our own time did a large part of humanity begin to suspect, or fear, that there may not be any answers.

If there aren't, man's mind has played the cruelest of jokes on him. It has lifted him above the other animals only to confront him with the awareness that his life is an absurd and ultimately futile struggle against nothingness.

To a materialist—and all of us are materialists to some degree—it seems odd that men should suffer agony of mind in this era of superabundance.

Never before have so many had so much. But the proliferation of things has only deepened the sense of emptiness which afflicts millions of men and women.

Never before have our achievements been so dazzling. We are able now to traverse continents in a few hours, to orbit the earth, to walk upon the moon. Yet our technological successes have only heightened our bitter frustration at being unable to abolish war and poverty.

Never before have we possessed such marvelous means of communication. A man can sit in New York and watch an Olympic meet in Tokyo. He can dial a telephone in Boston and be instantly connected with an office in San Francisco. He is inundated daily with information about news events, near and far. But he often cannot communicate with his own wife across the dinner table, or find out what his children are doing when they go out at night.

We speak of living in an affluent society. But it is also, even more conspicuously, an alienated society. Aware of our interdependency, hungry for meaningful human relationships, we nevertheless find ourselves shouting epithets and accusations across the gaps which separate race from race, class from class, generation from generation.

What has brought us to this unhappy state?

The great Jewish philosopher Will Herberg says we are victims of insidious intellectual currents which have undermined our confidence in the meaningfulness of human existence.

One of these currents is relativism, which Dr. Herberg defines as "the creeping conviction that there is no such thing as truth or right, but only the varying beliefs of varying cultures, each apparently justified in its own terms."

Another is secularism—the belief that there is no reality higher or more enduring than the physical universe, no realm of being beyond that which can be verified and measured by the methods of science.

These ideas—which are merely hypotheses, not demonstrated truths—have so permeated our culture that they condition nearly everyone's thinking, whether he realizes it or not.

A person surrounded by such a culture may take up arms against it, affirming in his own life the eternal truths and values it denies. But this is an exceptional response, requiring extraordinary resources of courage and conviction. The majority of people find it easier and more natural to accept the world view which is dominant in their environment. If that world view leaves no room for God, they perforce try to live without God.

This, however, is not as easy as it may seem to one newly arrived in the spiritual wasteland of atheism. For with God goes whatever hope man may have for escaping the sense of meaninglessness which hangs over a life circumscribed by inexorable death.

"The existentialist finds it very troublesome that God does not exist," says Jean-Paul Sartre, "because with him disappears all possibility of finding values in an intelligible world."

The consequences of a purely materialistic world view also have been spelled out by another honest atheist, Bertrand Russell:

"Man is the product of causes which had no prevision of the end they were achieving. His origin, his growth, his hopes and fears, his loves and beliefs, are but the outcome of accidental collocations of atoms. No fire, no heroism, no intensity of thought or feelings can preserve an individual life beyond the grave. All the labors of the ages, all the devotion, all the inspiration, all the noonday brightness of human genius, are destined to extinction in the vast death of the solar system."

Some men can live with that bleak philosophy. But many cannot.

Dr. Viktor Frankl, successor to Sigmund Freud as professor of psychiatry at the University of Vienna, says vast numbers of people today are suffering from severe neuroses because they cannot endure life in "an existential vacuum."

"It is an inherent tendency in man to reach out for meanings to fulfill and for values to actualize," says Dr. Frankl. "In contrast to animals, man is not told by his instincts what he must do. And in contrast to man in former times, he is no longer told by his conditions and values what he ought to do.

"The result is a worldwide phenomenon—more and more patients are crowding our clinics with the complaint of an inner emptiness, the sense of a total and ultimate meaning-lessness of life."

★ Questions to ponder or discuss

Is this a fair description of the way a lot of people seem to feel today?

Do *you* feel that life is meaningless?

Is Sartre right in saying that men cannot attribute any ultimate value or significance to their existence if they give up belief in God?

29 ☀ *Eight Little Words*

Eight little words could enormously improve the quality of American life.

The words are "sir," "ma'am," "please," "thank you," and "in my opinion."

If each of us made a point of using them on every possible occasion, we'd stop irritating each other so much.

Too many people today seem to think courtesy is an optional frill. It's not. It's an essential lubricant of human relations. Without it, friction quickly generates excessive heat.

Take "sir" and "ma'am" for example.

To employ these terms of address is not a sign of subservience. It's a way of saying to another person: "I respect your dignity as a human being."

Black people who are sensitive to any suggestion of inferior status may shrink from using these words in speaking to white people. That's understandable. But there's no reason why white people cannot say "sir" and "ma'am" to black people.

The courtesy eventually will be reciprocated. In the meantime, if things are a bit one-sided, perhaps it's time the shoe was on the other foot.

"Please" and "thank you" are demulcent words in any human encounter, and they can be particularly helpful in reducing friction between parents and children. The wise parent doesn't try to extract these words from his offspring by compulsion. He sets an example by using them himself. To say "please" to a child—or any other person in a dependent or subordinate role, such as an employee or servant—converts a demand into a request. "Thank you" is a way of saying, "I also am dependent on you."

Everyone wants to feel needed and valued. "Please" and "thank you" convey this feeling better than almost anything you can say.

"In my opinion" is the least used but potentially most helpful phrase of all.

We have all fallen into the habit of speaking too dogmatically. We say, in effect, "I know what I'm talking about, Buster, and if you don't see it my way you're just too stupid to understand."

That kind of arrogant speech will produce nothing but irritation, whether it's directed at your wife, your children, your neighbor, a political opponent, or the guy sitting next to you on the bus who dares to differ with you about politics or football.

But if you precede or follow your pronouncements with the defusing phrase, "in my opinion," a useful dialogue frequently can result. These three words acknowledge that the other person may have a different view of the matter, that he's as entitled to his view as you are to yours, and that it's at least possible he's right and you're wrong.

Perhaps if we abandon the illusion of infallibility, we can begin to communicate with each other and rebuild the spirit of mutual tolerance which is necessary to the harmonious functioning of a free society.

In my opinion, that is.

★ Questions to ponder or discuss

Two men are expounding different viewpoints on a subject you know little about. One seems very sure of himself, and makes strong, categorical statements. The other makes his points quietly, sprinkling his conversation with such phrases as "I may be wrong . . ." or "it seems to me. . . ." Which one would you find more persuasive?

How many times today did you say "thank you" to someone? Would the number be larger if you had made a deliberate effort to find occasions on which you could sincerely and legitimately express appreciation?

Can you think of other words or phrases that have a lubricating effect on interpersonal frictions?

30 ☀ *Are You Tired, Too?*

"Let us not become tired of doing good."

St. Paul addressed that admonition to Christians in Galatia nineteen centuries ago.

It could be appropriately readdressed to contemporary Americans of all faiths.

A perceptive observer commented recently that a great many Americans who are essentially kind and decent folk seem to be suffering from "compassion fatigue."

It's a good phrase. Think on it for a minute.

Webster defines compassion as "sympathetic consciousness of others' distress, together with a desire to alleviate it."

If you feel sorry for a person in need, that's pity. If you care enough about his troubles to try to help, that's compassion.

Fatigue is defined as "weariness from exertion, . . . the temporary loss of power to respond induced by continued stimulation."

Compassion fatigue, therefore, is a condition in which your capacity for sympathy has been exhausted by overuse.

When you consider all of the human suffering—at home and abroad—to which men of good will have tried to respond during the past quarter century, it is not very surprising that some of us are beginning to display symptoms of compassion fatigue.

Among the external symptoms, two in particular are noteworthy.

The first is a tendency to curtail contributions to worthy causes. You find yourself saying no to people who ask you to give money or time to help others.

The second is a growing readiness to accept any explanation of human misery which implies that the poor and oppressed have no one to blame but themselves.

You don't have to worry about how human beings can live on $50 a month in public assistance if you can believe that everyone on the welfare rolls is a deadbeat who's too lazy to work.

Like most ailments, spiritual and physical, compassion fatigue is easier to diagnose than to treat. It does not yield to exhortation or condemnation—even when self-administered. Flogging a tired conscience just makes it all the wearier.

Nor can the problem be solved by taking a "vacation from kindness" in which you tune out everyone else's troubles and wallow unabashedly in selfishness.

Each time you take that way out, you'll find it a little harder to return to the fray, and one day you'll just stay in your little cocoon of self-concern.

The only real cure for compassion fatigue is the one prescribed by the Bible. When you feel your wellsprings of mercy drying up, turn for refreshment to the source of all love.

"Love comes from God," says the First Epistle of John. It goes on to say that we are able to love each other only because the spirit of God acts in us and through us, whether we know it or not.

And therein lies the great purpose of prayer. It is not a gimmick whereby men wheedle favors from a capricious deity, but a channel whereby the all-encompassing love of a gracious God may pour into human hearts, washing away their fatigue, renewing their capacity to care.

★ Questions to ponder or discuss

The Urban Coalition has adopted as its motto: "Give a damn." Do you? About what?

Have the news media contributed to compassion fatigue by overusing their power to stir our emotions?

Do you sometimes feel that your natural sympathy for the suffering is being rather cynically manipulated by people who are trying to raise money or whip up popular support for a cause?

A wise Scottish preacher, George MacDonald, said there is nothing more dangerous to the soul than to indulge in the emotion of "feeling sorry" without trying to take some concrete action to help the person or relieve the situation that has engendered your sympathy. Why is this true?

31 ☀ *Go On—Get Mad*

St. Paul listed anger as one of the "works of the flesh" which Christians should strive to overcome.

Pope Gregory the Great called it one of the "seven deadly sins."

The author of Ecclesiastes warned that "anger lodges in the bosom of fools."

And then there are all of the things Jesus said in the Sermon on the Mount about turning the other cheek, forgiving those who wrong you, loving your enemies.

Considering the weight of this testimony, it is small wonder many people have gained the impression that it's unchristian ever to get good and mad.

But that is a grievous oversimplification.

For the Bible also speaks in many places of "righteous anger."

Jesus offers a classic example of what righteous anger is like. The Gospels make clear that he often displayed blazing indignation at hypocrisy, injustice, and selfishness. The third chapter of Mark, for example, tells how nit-picking Pharisees complained once when Jesus had healed a sick man on the sabbath day. Mark 3:5 says that Jesus "looked round about on them with anger, being grieved for the hardness of their hearts." (KJV)

On another occasion, Jesus was so incensed by the sight of racketeers preying on pilgrims in the very courtyard of the temple that he seized a whip and drove the rascals out.

Indeed, the whole career of Jesus attests to his strong conviction that it is far worse to be apathetic about wrong inflicted *on others* than to be angry about it.

In the preceding sentence the phrase "on others" is italicized because it is the key to the distinction between sinful anger and righteous anger.

"The first characteristic of righteous anger is that it is inspired and animated by unselfish considerations," says Dr. Norman V. Hope of Princeton Theological Seminary. "Far too often, our anger is rooted in selfishness, however we may try to hide this under noble motives. It is, at bottom, little more than personal resentment, born of some private injury or slight.'

But Jesus never spoke an angry word when he was personally mistreated. He even spoke kindly of the men who nailed him to the cross. His indignation was aroused only over wrong done to others, particularly the weak and helpless.

An English theologian, Canon R. E. C. Browne of Manchester Cathedral, observes that "a man of deep love and loyalties is more likely to be angry than one who cares little for any person or institution."

"Christianity does not say that Christians are never to be angry," says Canon Browne. "It would be subhuman for anyone not to be moved to anger by cruelty, deceit, treachery, or readiness to defraud or destroy the weak."

Again, however, there is the danger of oversimplifying. For even unselfish anger on behalf of others may be wrong if it is accompanied by a vengeful or vindictive spirit against individuals. The commandment of Christ is that we love all persons, even the most sinful and unlovely.

We may hate the sin, but we can never, in the name of Christ, hate the sinner.

★ Questions to ponder or discuss

Can you recall any recent occasion on which you were quite angry? What prompted your anger—a wrong inflicted on you, or a wrong done to someone else?

Are there social conditions or political situations that make you angry?

What are you *doing* about these things other than fuming in wrath?

Under what circumstances would you feel justified in seeking vengeance against a person who had done you wrong? Do you think Jesus would agree?

32 ☀ *Know When to Keep Quiet*

The Bible says there is "a time to keep silence, and a time to speak."

Knowing when it's time to keep silence is a difficult art, mastered by very few people.

Most of us manage in the course of our lives to get into a vast amount of trouble by missing golden opportunities for keeping our mouths shut.

Sometimes it's anger or malice or deliberate guile that prompts us to say things that would have been better left unsaid.

Quite often, however, it is simply a case of being nervous, ill at ease, or overanxious to please. Lacking the poise to keep silence, we find ourselves seeming to agree with sentiments we actually abhor, or revealing information we should have kept confidential.

This obviously is a human weakness of very long standing, for there are many references to it in parts of the Bible that were written two or three thousand years ago.

In the Psalms, the tongue is likened to a sharp sword and a carelessly wielded razor. The prophet Jeremiah added another military metaphor: an uncurbed tongue is "a cruel arrow."

The book of Proverbs lists seven things that are "detestable" to God, and three of them are related to speech: a false tongue, a false witness telling a pack of lies, one who stirs up quarrels among brothers.

Proverbs abounds with other warnings of the mischief that can be set in train by words:

"The babbling of a fool brings ruin near."

"He who conceals hatred has lying lips, and he who utters slander is a fool."

"When words are many, transgression is not lacking."

"He who restrains his lips is prudent."

"A perverse tongue falls into calamity."

But it is in the New Testament, and specifically in the Epistle of James, that we find the most trenchant comments about this ancient human weakness for talking when we ought to be listening.

"All of us often make mistakes," James says. "The person who never makes a mistake in what he says is perfect."

To anyone inclined to regard careless speech as a minor matter, James offers the reminder that a huge forest can be set ablaze by a tiny spark.

"And the tongue is like a fire," he says. "It is a world of wrong, occupying its place in our bodies and spreading evil through our whole being. . . .

"Man is able to tame, and has tamed, all other creatures— wild animals and birds, reptiles and fish. But no man has ever been able to tame the tongue. It is evil and uncontrollable, full of deadly poison. We use it to give thanks to our Lord and Father, and also to curse our fellow men, created in the likeness of God. . . .

"My brothers! This should not happen!"

121

★ Questions to ponder or discuss

Do you find it difficult to control your tongue?

How many times in the past week have you said things which you later wished you had not said?

In your opinion, which is worse: to tell a lie, or to spread malicious gossip?

Which is worse: to tell an outright barefaced lie, or to mislead someone by skillfully manipulating statements that are technically true?

Which is worse: to curse someone in a violent outburst of anger, or to put him down coolly with subtle digs and innuendos?

33 ☀ *Every Day Is Thanksgiving Day*

"It is good to give thanks to the Lord," the Bible declares. Why?

What purpose is served when a human creature turns in gratitude to his Creator?

The wrong answer is that rites of thanksgiving are necessary to appease a touchy deity. It is an insult to God to treat him like a stingy giver who may cut off his benefactions if we fail to display proper appreciation.

It's amazing how many "religious" people seem to think of thanksgiving as an onerous duty, to be undertaken out of prudential regard for the divine wrath which may fall upon those who neglect it.

Jesus rebuked this attitude. He reminded his disciples that even human parents, with all their shortcomings, usually are unselfish enough to provide for their children's welfare without demanding anything—including expressions of gratitude —in return. God, he added, is infinitely more willing than the best of earthly fathers to give without strings.

Another widespread attitude views thanksgiving as an act in which we acknowledge, gladly or grudgingly as the case may be, that there may be some good things in our lives which are not directly traceable to our own hard work and other virtues.

The pitfall in this approach is that those who take it are apt to give God credit for good luck while nursing secret grudges against him for any bad luck that befalls them. In either event, they run the risk of attributing to express divine volition events which result from the random workings of a natural order in which God has seen fit, for our soul's health, to leave room for chance, accidents, uncertainty, danger, and pain, as well as undeserved prosperity, health, happiness, love, truth, and beauty.

If gratitude is not an emotion to be conjured up by "counting our blessings" (and trying to forget our troubles), what is it?

The biblical answer is that true thanksgiving—the only kind that can possibly matter a whit to God or to us—is a spontaneous response of our hearts to the conviction that God loves us. Its spirit is perfectly expressed in the ancient Jewish prayer found at the beginning of several Old Testament Psalms:

> *O give thanks to the Lord, for he is good;*
> *his steadfast love endures for ever.*

Another way of putting it is that thanksgiving is a celebration of the goodness and mercy of God, on the part of one who has experienced that goodness and mercy at first hand in his own life.

It should be noted that belief in God's kindness is not confined to persons who are conspicuously endowed with material "blessings." On the contrary, it very often is in the midst of pain, trouble, need, or despair that a person becomes most certainly aware of the inexplicable love in whose presence all else seems unimportant.

It is indeed good to give thanks to the Lord. For thanksgiving is the other face of faith. You can't have one without the other.

★ Questions to ponder or discuss

Take it all in all, would you say that God has been good to you?

In what ways?

What is the *best* thing God has done for you—the thing for which you are *most* thankful?

Experienced Christians sometimes find themselves thanking God for their troubles. Is this a nutty thing to do, or can you see how it might make sense?

34 ※ Dryness

"In every earnest life there are weary flats to tread, with the heavens out of sight—no sun, no moon—and not a tint of light upon the path below; when the only guidance is the faith of brighter hours, and the secret Hand we are too numb and dark to feel."

Those words were written by the nineteenth-century theologian James Martineau.

They describe a condition that is painfully familiar to every pilgrim.

St. Teresa called it "the dark night of the soul." Other saints, less poetic, have referred to it simply as spiritual dryness.

Their testimony is unanimous that the darkness is apt to fall, suddenly and unpredictably, on those who have walked for years in the light of faith, as well as on those who have only recently set their feet upon the pathway.

It is always a dismaying experience, even to veterans who have been through it many times before and know that it will pass. In fact, it is probably more distressing to true saints than to the rest of us. The better you know God, the more you miss the sense of his presence when it is withdrawn for a while.

Why does God let this happen to those who love him? Is it punishment for spiritual pride, a way of reminding us that we can never be good on our own, that we cannot be faithful and loving for a single hour unless he gives us the grace to do so? Some of the saints have thought so.

Sometimes, also, "dryness" may be brought on by sheer fatigue—including the emotional fatigue which results from caring a great deal about others.

The New Testament records that Christ himself frequently found it necessary to disengage from the rat race of daily life and withdraw into a quiet place for a spell of battery-recharging. If the most self-giving person who ever lived could not go on indefinitely without running dry of feelings, it is surely presumptuous for the rest of us to expect to do so.

George MacDonald, the nineteenth-century Scottish cleric whose writings had so great an influence on C. S. Lewis, suggested that intervals of spiritual aridity are necessary to preserve free will.

"God does not, by the instant gift of his Spirit, make us always feel right, desire good, love purity, aspire after him and his will," MacDonald wrote. "He wants to make us in his own image, *choosing* the good, *refusing* the evil. How could he effect this if he were *always* moving us from within, as he does at divine intervals?"

The wise old Scot warned against "frantic efforts to rouse" lost feelings.

"Troubled soul, thou are not bound to feel," he said. "God loves thee whether thou feelest or not. Thou canst not love when thou wilt, but thou are bound to fight the hatred in thee to the last.

"Try not to feel good when thou are not good, but cry to him who is good. He changes not because thou changest. Nay, he has an especial tenderness of love towards thee for that thou are in the dark and hast no light. . . .

"Fold the arms of thy faith, and wait in the quietness until

127

light goes up in thy darkness. Fold the arms of thy faith, I say, but not of thy action. Bethink thee of something that thou oughtest to do, and go to do it, if it be but the sweeping of a room, or the preparing of a meal, or a visit to a friend.

"Heed not thy feelings: do thy work."

★ Questions to ponder or discuss

Have you experienced periods of spiritual dryness?
What did you do about it?

In the light of what psychosomatic medicine has taught us about the impact of the body on the mind and spirit, is it legitimate to say that avoiding excessive fatigue—getting enough recreation and rest—is an important *religious* duty?